THE SUN'S NOT BROKEN, A CLOUD'S JUST IN THE WAY

On Child-Centered Teaching

Sydney Gurewitz Clemens

Gryphon House
Mt. Rainier, Maryland

The quotations from WINNIE-THE-POOH and THE HOUSE AT POOH CORNER by A. A. Milne are reprinted by permission of the publisher, E. P. Dutton, Inc.

The article, "School Boards and Community Power: The Irony of Professionalism," is reprinted in the Appendix with the permission of the author, Dr. L. Harmon Ziegler

Library of Congress Cataloging in Publication Data

Clemens, Sydney Gurewitz, 1939-
    The sun's not broken.

    Includes bibliographies and index.
    1. Clemens, Sydney Gurewitz, 1939-   . 2. Teachers
--California--Biography. 3. Teachers--New York (State)--
Biography. 4. Education, Urban--New York (N.Y.)--Case
studies. 5. Education, Urban--California--San Francisco
--Case studies. 6. Afro-American children--Education--
New York (N.Y.)--Case studies. 7. Afro-American children
--Education--California--San Francisco--Case studies.
I. Title.
LA2317.C53A37 1983   371.1'0092'4 [B]   84-3818
ISBN 0-87659-109-8 (pbk.)

ISBN Number 0-87659-109-8

Published by Gryphon House, Inc.
3706 Otis Street
Mt. Rainier MD 20712, USA

Thanks

Before Gryphon House became the publisher of this book it languished on my shelves, making me nervous. In the Spring of 1983, under the influence of Neal Powers, Marna Cohen, Ed Roecker and Ron Jones (each of them amazing and nurturant) I decided to publish it myself. I wrote letters to a lot of my friends asking for contributions so as to pay the printer, and everybody helped. Here are the names of my wonderful sponsors:

Donna Levis, Judy Hubner, Barbara Selvidge, Karen Prindle, Spencer Prindle, Helen Sobell, Ron Clemens, Alan D. Sklar, Carl Cheney, G. Murray Branch, Elissa Matross, Edith Garduk, Charles Garrigues, Emma and Lincoln Chu, Lisbeth Jones, David Levitov, Margaret Bean, Yuko and Comer Marshall, Terry Virgason, Arnie and Margo Miller, and Lore and Don Rasmussen.

This book is dedicated to my mother, Helen Sobell, whose example of how to live a full life has always inspired me. Because Helen takes risks and learns new and hard things she does some of my work for me, giving me a gift of time.

And to my children, Alexander Jeremy Clemens and Jennifer Martine Clemens, who experienced the burden of my going off and writing when they'd have preferred my company, a big hugging thanks.

Contents

Introduction

When we asked Pooh what the opposite of an Introduction was, he said "The what of a what?" which didn't help us as much as we had hoped, but luckily Owl kept his head and told us that the opposite of an Introduction, my dear Pooh, was a Contradiction; and, as he is very good at long words, I am sure that that's what it is.

—The House at Pooh Corner

I've been working with black four-year-olds in inner-city settings for twelve years—eight of them at Burnett Prekindergarten in the Hunters Point section of San Francisco. The class, one of 30 housed in public schools in poor neighborhoods, was an ESEA Title I project funded by the federal government. At first the prekindergarten was in the kindergarten wing of a fourth to sixth grade school. Later, on the pretext of economy, the big school was shut down, but our parents and staff kept the prekindergarten alive for another five years through pressure on the school board and publicity about the program's value to the community.

I experienced great autonomy at Burnett, thanks in large part to the design and management of the program by Madelon Halpern, who appreciated my style and let me teach to the rhythm of my own drummer. And each day at Burnett I felt the support of excellent paraprofessionals: Ron Clemens for a year, Sondra Dunkerson for three, and Katherine Primes for the last five. Katherine is the other adult in the classroom in this book. She is employed as a teacher's aide, but her way of working with me has been to see to it that I am relaxed and calm. She models maturity, black pride and inner peace to all around her. Without her backing I couldn't have taken the chances that have given me some of my best teaching moments.

Readers interested in book writing, editing, and publishing are urged to read the Epilogue: How this book came to be written. Let me only say here that I am lucky to be the friend of talented people, and to have had so much capable help. Ron used to say that all our kids were gifted; our job was to find out just which child had which gift. Working with these three fine people gave me a chance to design many ways to uncover children's gifts. I hope this book supports your work as they have supported mine. If you are interested in telling me how you solve the problems that come up, or in helping to make future editions of this book truer through your perceptions, write to me through Gryphon House.

1
Feelings and Learning

This book is about a few grownups and a lot of children I've known, and how we move together toward strength and reality. Consider a child like Reba, who didn't believe that the big people would take care of her. In a dangerous world she debated every choice we made for her, frantically trying to take responsibility for everything, like a baby carrying itself in its arms. I was dismayed by her pain and her rigid reliance on defenses that didn't protect her. One day I confronted her: "But Reba, I'm stronger than you are. Big people are supposed to take care of little people." She replied, "I'm REALLY bigger than you!" I put my hands around the waist of this regular-sized four-year-old and lifted her above my head, holding her there for a while. Then I put her down and said, "Now you lift me."

She cried and cried and let me rock her and tell her it was all right for her to be little. If I could be big for her, she could put the baby down.

1

Can they solve it themselves? When to intervene

What does Christopher Robin do in the mornings? He learns. He becomes Edu-
cated. He instigorates—I think that is the word he mentioned, but I may be referring
to something else—he instigorates Knowledge.

—The House at Pooh Corner

Close your eyes and imagine a group of young children. Were they in motion? I find that when I want to teach something to a child this generally interrupts what she or he is already doing.

Teachers teach for the wrong reasons much of the time. We teach what we've been taught, what will keep children busy, or what's easy for us. But we have no business interrupting a child unless we have reason to believe we're meeting that child's needs and interests.

Once, visiting a classroom, I found myself growing upset and angry. The teacher was punitive, restrictive, and making inappropriate choices of things to do with the children. Unsupervised, they would learn more from the materials and their interactions alone than they could with their teacher bossily interrupting. Social critic Paul Goodman makes this point most dramatically in his novel, *The Empire City*. Its hero is educated in the streets, by choice, since on registration day for kindergarten, he "looked sharp and stole the records."

We need to know why we're intervening. A good teacher constantly struggles to improve the quality and timeliness of intervention. Let us consider when to intervene—if at all.

Teachers don't choose when learning will occur, since children are learning all the time. A teacher decides when to let the children explore on their own and when to support and broaden their experience. If we can examine and refine our motives for intervention we will go far toward becoming teachers who set children free.

When you teach, eliminate noise, clutter, and distraction. The resulting quiet makes for high quality interventions. Analyze the parts of the task and the student's style (conservative? courageous? visual? auditory? kinesthetic?) then

3

guide the child with a suitable program through the activity. You want to provide enough adventure so it isn't boring and enough security so it isn't scary. The optimum mix is different for each person.

It helps me be clear about intervening if I name the principle I'm serving, so as to intervene only with cause, and not to prove my power over the children.

Interventions for the sake of safety require the grownup to move as well as talk. If Lukash isn't careful about climbing the ladder to the tree house, I climb up and carry him bodily to safety, then review the rules. Having made it clear what a disaster his falling would be, I then entrust him to his instinct of self-preservation.

In our prekindergarten we let children climb as high as they wish, because our experience is that they know very well just how high they can go. However, for safety's sake we interrupt a child who is goading another to climb high. Each of us must decide alone, without help from our friends, just how high to climb. Interestingly, children descend a slope, stairway, or escalator with less self-knowledge than they use climbing up. Adults in charge of children under six do well to be at the front of the group at such times.

For the sake of community health, we teach children to cover coughs and not to return food, or utensils they have licked, to serving bowls. We teach them to assess the weather and dress accordingly. Allergic children are expected to know and to avoid things that make them react.

In the name of social justice, we don't allow the children to exclude others from play because of sex, race, or age. We override Deena when she says, "Only girls can play in this house," or Thomas when he says, "Girls can't climb up this treehouse." We give them language to fight this exclusion: "This school is for *everybody*." And: "Dr. Martin Luther King said you have to be friends with *all* the children." We help them look clearly at race as coloration, not virtue. Racial epithets are treated like any other cruelty, by removing the offender till the victim is ready to accept the child again. If some children feel that another is too little to play well, we tell them to let the littler one try and then all decide together. Often this results in a new, deeper respect for that child.

Yet we never tell children how they must feel. I have come to believe that while we must behave well toward others, it is wrong to tell anyone what his or her feelings are, or what to feel. It's all right to help find names for feelings— "Are you feeling angry or sad?" but not to command them—"Tell her you're sorry." Each of us must learn to speak of our own feelings, and to inquire about the feelings of others. Hence I will say, "I feel angry when I see you hit Amanda" or "Please look at Leslie's face and see how she's doing."

We intervene when children are discourteous. I can tolerate children disliking each other, but I expect them to avoid rather than to irritate those they don't like, especially because today's enemy so often becomes tomorrow's best friend.

It's good to invite a child who has just done something, anything, for the first time ever, to repeat the experience. If you explore this, you'll see how important it is, because the children will often choose to repeat. They find real satisfaction in knowing they can do something better each time. You can encourage this by intervening to remind children that they may repeat.

We intervene in property arguments, particularly when the property belongs to neither of the parties, nor to Katherine or me, but to the school, and is meant for all of us to share.

Jerome Bruner says there's an intellectually honest way to teach anything to anyone at any age. This implies that you never tell children, no matter how young, that babies come from storks. Give them part of the true story or an overview, but don't lie, evade, or postpone.

After we've given the children good information for a while, they learn that we are reliable, we have knowledge and like to share it with them. Then they start bringing us material they feel is incomplete, distorted, or strange. When they know we won't evade or lie to them, they trust us.

Wesley wanted to know "Are earthquakes real?" We discussed this in the circle and some other children wanted to know if an earthquake was a monster.

Lisa told about monsters one day in the circle. Shawn told her, "Monsters ain't real, they just betend." She said her Uncle James tells her about monsters. Ivan advised: "Tell your uncle, 'Doan tell me no more 'bout monsters.' "

Georgia walked in one morning and said, "Sydney, I gotta talk to you. My Big Mama (grandmother) died yesterday, and my Mama's all cryin'." I asked if she'd like me to rock her, and we did that for a little while, and then she went off to join a group building a train track. Later, at reading, she said she wanted the word "grumpy."

Another time George went to the park with Polly, a student teacher, and five other children. George (Black) said to Polly (White), "Shut up, honky." Then he watched her for a reaction, but she didn't react. Then he seriously asked her if it was wrong to say that. She told him that people use words like honky to hurt each other, and that he'd be better off using other words.

When, after days and days of fog and gloom, Hamid told me "The sun's broken", I responded first to the poetic insight of his observation: "It really feels that way, Hamid." Then I went on to correct his information: "You know, the sun isn't a machine. It doesn't break. Clouds get in the way so we can't see or feel the sun, but they'll go away again and we'll see the sun some more."

I try to convey the same honesty about creative work, instead of slipping into a pattern of praising equally all the artwork the children do. I praise drawings and paintings and collages and clay work that reflect emotion, interest, or care. But when a child brings me slapdash work I say, "It's okay, but I don't think that's your best work." So the children believe the compliment when it does come, and know I tell them what I really think.

The skillful and respectful teacher interrupts children's natural learning only for good reason. If the group is large, there may scarcely be time to make these appropriate interventions. If the group is (mercifully) small, one can best spend extra time observing or joining in the play.

When the children see me painting at the easel or jumping rope or dancing, they find out I'm not just a grownup, but a person. As they realize my fun in playing, the distance between us narrows, making our life together easier and more pleasant.

Lissa Matross, a caucasian friend who teaches in Chinatown, tells me that during the first weeks of school she "eats" a fair amount of playdough and sand—so the children decide she's pretty silly, and they lose some of their fear of her as a stranger. She says that by late October she can cut down on her sand and playdough diet. Behind this whimsy is great respect for children.

Other teaching friends, Yuko Marshall and Dan McGettigan, regularly took their class to a park where there was no equipment. At first the children were disoriented, thinking there was nothing to do. The adults got busy preparing food, and in time the children began to lead each other into forays of discovery. They climbed trees and fences and hills; hid from each other in the bushes; chased each other; collected sticks and squashed snails; and discovered pine cones, pebbles, feathers and junk of all sorts. They brought treasures back, and came for help when others were stuck in hard-to-get-out-of places. The adults limited them to a large but visible area. This was excellent teaching: nonintervention to let children find their own fun.

Sometimes a community is ready to celebrate together. Especially if the children have been making gains through great effort, they need times for dancing, singing, parading, and playing music. The teacher creates such times, supporting children's impulses to celebrate.

Once the doctor came and gave everybody rubella shots. We dealt with everybody's fears and applauded everybody's bravery, and finally got done. The children were very interested when we told them that there's medicine in the shot needles. Then we had a peanut party and sang songs. After all the anxiety that went before, it made us feel better to relax. And feeling relaxed is a really good outcome of any intervention.

2

Taking time for feelings:
Finding support at school

Then suddenly he was dreaming. He was at the East Pole, and it was a very cold pole with the coldest sor. of snow and ice all over it. He had found a bee-hive to sleep in, but there wasn't room for his legs, so he had left them outside. And Wild Woozles, such as inhabit the East Pole, came and nibbled all the fur off his legs to make nests for their Young. And the more they nibbled, the colder his legs got, until suddenly he woke up with an Ow! and there he was, sitting in his chair with his feet in the water, and water all round him!

—Winnie-the-Pooh

The traditional school curriculum has no slot for affective learning; there is no subject area before high-school hygiene or college psychology. There is no academic sequence teaching little children that when your friend's uptight, it's a good idea to rub her shoulders, or massage her feet or hands. Perhaps one reason adults have so much energy to spend on the human potential movement is that in their childhoods, when these problems of fear and power and love first became compelling, the curriculum was confined to the three R's. We can use the power of children's emotions as the basis for a strong language program, helping them to be more expressive and fluent. There's no stronger motivation for any of us than the wish to recognize, understand, and gracefully express our feelings.

Getting the Talking Started

At four, children's strong feelings have to do with power and control over their environment and their relationships: siblings, dreams, eating, sex, monsters, superheroes, friendships, and toileting. We want to begin to discuss these topics as early in the year as we can, so we assess children's readiness to discuss feelings publicly. If such language is still difficult for many, we talk about feelings only in very small groups, or alone with a child as occasion warrants. Opportunities to do this often arise around the issues of sharing and of exclusion.

Our children learn about sharing at school, if they haven't at home. You can't just grab what you want and play with it; others have rights too, no matter how strong your feelings. I wish I had a nickel for every time I've told a child, "You can't have it now, but you *will* get a turn." This kind of promise must be solemnly kept, and all adults working with a group of children have to know about any such promise. Once I saw a teacher promise the children that they all would be allowed to paint that day. Her co-teacher was out of the room, getting supplies. Later, I heard the co-teacher tell a child, "You'll get a turn tomorrow, dear. There's not enough time for everyone to paint today."

Children who are excluded by their classmates feel awful. Much of the pain can be avoided by giving children different words. So, when Ivan says, "Bet you can't do this!", I say "Ivan, say 'Can you do this?' " And when Amanda says, "Terry, I'm not gonna be your friend," I say "Tell Terry, 'I can have all the friends I want.' " As the children become more articulate about their feelings, we begin to talk them over in our group meetings.

Healing

Schools defeat learning by emphasizing intellectual work at the expense of emotional clarity. I learned this from Ann Brown when we worked together at the Discovery Room for Children, a day-care center we founded in New York City in 1969. We were both early childhood teachers, wanting to work in a child-centered, racially integrated setting. We were also both parents of nursery-age children, and tired of the search for good programs.

We exchanged a great deal that year, since I knew a lot about teaching children's minds, and she knew all about teaching their hearts. In the years since then I've found myself continuing to discover sensitivities Ann stimulated long ago. (Ann has since founded the Newark Center for Creative Learning in Delaware, a solid, productive place for teachers and children, serving nursery through eighth grade.)

People in groups are often at a loss as to how to behave in the face of someone else's pain. In the fall, when the children hear another child crying, they don't get involved. Some children's faces reflect soft hearts, and they look pained, but even they don't know what to do. In September and October I say to Daphne near me, "Look, Lukash's crying. Run over and put your arm around him." If Daphne looks puzzled, we go over together and I drape her arm around Lukash, and pet Lukash with Daphne's hand. By January, the children comfort each other on their own. They bring the crying child to an adult only if it seems that a bandaid or other adult care is needed. If the crying is best mended with a hug, another child does the hugging. When Leslie has a nosebleed and must stay quiet for a while, Deena sits there too, for company. Thus they learn the joy of easing another's pain.

Once, teaching a workshop for teachers at a parochial school education fair, my group, studying "Language and Feelings in the Early Childhood Classroom," was tucked away in the nurse's office. A pregnant teacher found a seat on what appeared to be a sturdy cot. Just after I made the point that feelings are important enough to warrant interrupting lessons, the cot collapsed. It was terrific: the woman wasn't hurt at all, but because we all wanted to take care of her, we interrupted our important academic learning to take care of our feelings first.

Dreams and Power

The Senoi Indians of the Malay Peninsula are noted for good mental health, rooted, it seems, in the culture's sophisticated way of educating children through dreams (see Stewart, Bibliography I). The Senoi assume that people can change or control their dreams. Children are expected to tell their dreams each day to their elders, who then direct them to meet anger with courage or to give a present to someone they've offended in a dream. If a child reports a fearsome falling dream, the elders say, "What a wonderful dream. Next time you can fly to some wonderful place!"

The Centering Book by Gay Hendricks and Russel Wills, (see Bibliography I) devotes an entire chapter to step-by-step guidance on Senoi dreamwork with young children. Look into their work if you feel excited about these ideas.

Hearing the song, *You Tell Me Your Dream*, I was struck by the four-year-old sound of the line: "Mine was the best dream, because it was of you." At school the next day, when I taught the song, the children began to teach me about dreams.

They taught me that fours don't know where their dreams come from, that many fours think only bad dreams are dreams, that TV horror shows are a primary source of remembered dream material, and so, for some, the goal is to avoid dreaming.

Having learned a starting place, I teach them that dreams come from your mind. They try to tell me that dreams come from under the bed, from the closet, from anywhere external. To convince them to own their dreams is a struggle. After three or four discussions I got Ivan to concede that "Bad dreams come from your *stupid* brain!" He also surprised us by saying, "I wanted my dream to *live!*"

For four-year-olds who are coping with powerlessness, taking responsibility for their own dreams is a huge step. We teach that by talking to your dreams before you sleep, you can influence their content. We encourage the children to share good dream ideas: you could have a party, you could dream playing in the park, you could visit your grandma, you could dream your birthday. We suggest that if Frankenstein puts bad dream ideas in your head, you can tell the grownups you don't want to watch a scary movie, and go to another room away from the TV. Once again I begin appealing to parents, saying that I'm hearing all sorts of scary fantasies from their children, and want them to know my feeling that horror shows are seriously damaging.

The children are under no obligation to do what is suggested in these meetings. They don't usually tell us whether they talk to their dreams, but their continuing high interest in the subject leads me to believe they get something very nourishing from it, and I'm sure that those who need their monsters are in no way threatened by our information.

The language of these discussions is some of the most vivid we hear from the children. Here are dreams the children told us that give some idea of what wildness can come out:

Bernice: "I saw a monster behind my bed and he was yellow. He said he was coming to get Bernice. So he made me scared and I woke up."

Hal: "I saw a monster. He was upstairs in the kitchen and busted one of my windows with his hand. Then he ate all our soup up. Then he ate me up. I wasn't scared."

Deena: "I was scared of the monster, and I got in my Mama's bed."

Dinah: "A monster got in bed and slept with me. My bed was black when I got up."

Daphne: "Mommy was sleeping and then a blue flower came in the house."

Ivan: "I was in the hospital with my mother and she went home and I stole nine dollars from the bank and the police ran after me and I was dead!"

Thomas: "There was a dog in the garden. It ate our cabbage up. Then it ate our beans up. Then Daddy said, 'Run away big dog.' A cat ate the cabbage. Snails ate the greens. A gopher ate the lettuce and grass and sour grass."

Lukash: "It was a monster down my basement, shiny with black eyes. Ate my icebox. Then my Daddy got a gun and shot it".

Shabazz: "I heard somebody knock on the door. My Daddy woked up. And I saw a bird fly, a pigeon. And a monster came down. Pecked a wing on the head. A mosquito came down and stinged on there. My Daddy call the police. Write that down! My Daddy call the police. The police came and shot him with a gun. And they beat him up with a stick."

(Are you scared about his getting hurt?)

"My Daddy write words on the wall. He whup me; you won't show him my story?"

(I'll show you where we'll keep it.)

Leslie: "King Kong grabbed me and took me to his big blue house on a hill. He put me in his bed. I was in front and he was in the window. The ghost took me to his white house. It had a hill. He ran and put me in a car and took me home and ate me up. The ghost had a dog and left my bones for the dog."

We act out monster dreams. As Dinah tells us her dream she calls on every-body to help drive out the monster. All the children protect her, helping to change the dream. Leslie is the monster and creeps up on her. Then Dinah hollers: "Go away, monster, go away, I don't want you in my dream!" The dreamer can ask the other children to help with the hollering. (Thanks to Emily Beals-Nesmith for this idea.) Children tell each other what to say to the monster in the dream. "How could you make the dream better?" "What would you dream next time?" we ask the children. From this discussion come words for the reading program, which uses each child's feeling-laden words, since surely the name of the scary thing in your dream captions a real emotion.

We read and reread Mercer Mayer's *There's a Nightmare in my Closet*. Some children ask for this book, yet are reticent to tell their own dreams. I find that working with dreams in December and then reading the book once a month lets children tell what's new with their dreams.

Powerlessness

People who are four years old are neither innocent nor unaware. "I'm the King of the Mountain, and anything you can do, I can do better than you can." Most fours perceive all sorts of power relations in the world, and yet they them-selves control so very little power.

The children find themselves in a very frustrating situation, where they can imagine driving a car or an airplane, but their legs don't reach and anyway, the grownups won't let them do it. They can conceive of an earthquake, or a bomb, or a gun, and like grownups they cannot control these things. But they think adults are very powerful and can control anything. They've just begun to distin-guish the real people on TV from the Bionic Woman or Superman.

Susan called me a few days after her son Petey, in my class, began having tantrums. She said these had gone on ever since her husband, Ted, had left on a business trip. Had anything happened at the airport, I wondered. Well not really, she said. Ted had told Petey, "You're the man of the house now, son. I want you to take care of your mother." My gorge rose. "Well, you tell Petey that *you're* going to take care of *him*! You're a grown woman and he's a little boy and he's terrified of the responsibility his father handed him." Susan told him that, and the tantrums stopped.

Race

The basic training we give about race is about being a good person and feeling good about yourself and others . . . knowing you can help, share, take turns, etc. We make sure that the books we read and the language and pictures we use are multiracial and nonsexist.

Since we live in a biased society, it's essential to teach children positive ways of viewing diversity, to offset what they're likely to pick up on the street. I learned a neat way to teach skin color from Audrey Jones, a teacher who was my student at Lone Mountain College. Audrey's class built a chart where each child compared his or her skin color to the color of a food. When we tried it in our class, this is what came out:

Gene said, "My skin is like a hamburger."
Frank said, "My skin is the color of pineapple."
Pattia said, "My skin is the color of crab."
Tish said, "My skin is the color of yams."
Anna Fay said, "My skin's like fried chicken."
Lukash said, "My skin is the color of spaghetti."
Daphne said, "My skin is the color of chocolate."

Handling Mistakes

The children all exhibit some fear of what will happen when they do something wrong at school. The fear is not very intense, but their behavior is instructive. During the first week of school, Lukash broke one of the little plastic containers from the table where children play with water. I happened to see him break it, drop it on the ground, and set his face to look as if he didn't know about any broken toys. Leslie picked it up and gave it to me, saying, "He broke it." Everyone was worried. I seized the moment to teach how to handle breaking a toy. I said very slowly and carefully, "When a toy is broken, I want you to bring it to Katherine or me." Then I asked Amanda, standing nearby, "Tell me what I want you to do with a broken toy." She responded, "Throw it in the garbage." I said no, and repeated my question; she repeated her answer. Turning to Leslie, I asked the same question. Leslie looked puzzled, so Amanda came to her rescue, now that the pressure was off, saying sensibly, "You want us to bring it to a grownup."

While our homes are generally run for the convenience and comfort of adults, we can run schools to meet children's needs. The children learn this difference. Early in September, Amanda spilled some milk at snacktime and I told her to get the sponge from its place on the cart nearby. Together we tidied, cleaning the table and floor, and then I moved the damp chair away, replacing it with a dry one. Amanda put the sponge away and returned just in time to see me putting "her" chair at an empty table. She took this to mean that she was to sit alone, away from the group. She rejoined us only after I told her she was welcome at her old place at the table, on a dry chair.

The only way to deal with this kind of fear, since it's based on reality and experience, is to show children other alternatives. Your behavior can show children that there's another way a problem can be handled; there are different grownups in the world and they handle problems different ways; and at our school we can be freer to make mistakes or take risks than elsewhere.

I'm consistently patient with children when they spill milk and break cheap toys, but when Millie took drumsticks to our hand drums and broke all three in a minute, showing us that she knows what drumsticks are for, I was desolate and shared my sadness with her. I didn't punish her for it, however, since she had done it in ignorance or creativity, meaning no harm. To avoid this kind of tragedy we try to keep easily breakable toys where it takes an adult to get them, so big people can remind little ones how to handle them.

Millie

We teachers need to see the children grow more than they would if we didn't intervene. In order to perceive this growth, we must depart from customary teaching, to record and analyze, and plot, plan, and connive, sometimes even before a child has entered school.

When Millie was registered, (see also Part III, Chapter 1) we wrote this log:

Aunt brought Millie to register.

Child is beautiful, solid, face a tragic mask.

She didn't want to speak at all.

Mother had a "mental breakdown," and Millie lives with maternal grandmother.

Millie wouldn't tell me whether or not she wanted food until I put a chair at the table and began to lead her to it. Then she said, "NO!"

Her voice is very husky and she only emits speeches of one syllable.

Gave her markers and paper, but she wouldn't draw until I made a first mark on the paper. Liked to draw, used several colors.

Listened carefully to the interview and cried softly when I talked with her aunt about leaving her at school. Let me hold her a lot.

Katherine and I both feel that Millie may be seriously disturbed.

Aunt announced that she "has the most interest in children of anybody in the family."

Says Millie talks more to her than to the others.

We feel extreme poverty in this family.

When they left, I found that Rick, the young man who came with them, had carved his name into our styrofoam box holding the markers. Again, I sensed poverty.

Since Millie's speech development was poor, and she seemed to be emotionally adrift, lacking adult support, we started right away to plan for the help she needed. The day she registered, I arranged for Katherine and me to meet with our social worker, Amy Williams, to plan Millie's first day at school. Worried that separation from her family would upset her, we saw to it that Millie would experience success from the start, that she'd hear speech modelled many times before she was asked to produce it, and that she would have time alone with Katherine or me each day.

All of this was a little harder because Millie entered school in November, after other patterns were set, as children from disorganized families often do. We must be careful not to penalize them for the poor timing.

Our log records Millie's progress during the year. We can't sort out which gains belong to her determination to survive and which to our program for her. Nevertheless, I feel joy when I read in the October 23 log that Millie, acting as my messenger and repeating my words, told Dinah I wanted her to come in and read; that on October 27 she said, spontaneously, "I'm done" when she finished a painting; that early in November, when I told her I didn't like something she'd done, she said, "I said I'm sorry," using language to try to ease a tense situation. I'm excited to read that she was "blabbing" at the circle in mid-November, that by December she was reading 12 words (family names plus monster, school, ice cream, bike, nice, orange, and dress). That in December, too, one day she punched the pillow and kicked it, then asked to be rocked, then painted an all red painting, and then relaxed in the dollhouse. In January, punching the pillow, she was able to say "Rick, I'm mad at you. You made me cry." In February she angrily told Katherine when Lukash threw a pail at her, and I recorded that "She seems to be in love with language."

By year's end Millie read 24 words. At graduation she recited a poem with the others, and because we had a record of her progress we know we helped Millie grow. When a grown-up helps free a child's intelligence it feels wonderful to them both. This joy transfigures a classroom.

Our prekindergarten children all learn to read. (See Part II, Chapter 8.) Tragically, there are other children as old as twelve or even sixteen who've gone to school for a long time but can't read as many words as ours do. If children don't succeed with a task valued so highly in our culture, it's because at some level they see greater rewards for failure than for success. Adults tend to pay attention to negative behavior. Special teachers aren't hired to spend individual time with the children who read well, but on occasion they are asked to help children who are failing.

Millie is reported to have fallen on her head when she first tried walking, and then to have given up trying to walk till she was more than two years old. Ninety per cent of babies walk alone by 14 months, and most are encouraged by loving parents to get up and try again when they fall. For a child to have chosen resistance so early suggests that she was more rewarded for failure than for effort. Grownups who need a placid baby have to be very strong to stifle the baby's developmental urge to walk. During her year with us, Millie's family reported a couple of three- and four-week periods when "something was wrong with Millie's leg," and she had to be carried. She didn't come to school during these periods, and lost ground. When she returned, our nurse and doctor checked her legs, but none of us ever saw anything wrong with them. We gave her many opportunities to crawl and rock and climb, and to see that we admired how her legs worked.

Children like Millie, past the optimum point for learning something, have an arduous struggle. They need at least a safe space, where they can make mistakes without being devastated by them. And a grownup who encourages: "Oh, you didn't learn that. I didn't teach it well enough. Let's try again." These children require many repetitions of their lessons. They need to use painting, clay and block building to solve problems on a safe, nonverbal level before they try words.

Living Together in The School

In our room children don't have to like each other. They just have to live together decently.

After they've been with us a while we ask for certain social amenities. We insist that they all learn people's names, and that they talk face to face, looking into each other's eyes. Beyond that, if they cooperate and share, we don't fuss about manners. We've discovered that if we don't teach the children to call each other by name, many won't. So we use the Language Master machine to combine auditory and visual signals, taping a picture of a child to each card, and saying the name, very clearly, on the audio tape. The children like to use the machine, and some learn names this way. We also clap names rhythmically around the circle, to identify and honor each other. When Lukash finishes his private reading lesson with me I send him back out to the yard to send me Millie, and hold him responsible for seeing to it that Millie gets to me. If he hasn't learned who Millie is, Katherine will help him. (See also Part II, Chapter 7.)

When Amanda and Daphne were playing dominoes, and Daphne insisted on calling Amanda "Commander," I corrected her four or five times, and got Amanda to tell Daphne her name. I even had Lukash (who has speech problems of his own) tell her how to say "Amanda". I got tough and distant until Daphne had Amanda's name right; then I broke into cheers and praise.

One of the greatest releases in my life came when Ruth Dreiblatt told me I didn't have to like all the children I work with. And some years there is a child I don't like. But I teach them all, and take responsibility to see that they grow. I take special care to study a child I don't like. This invariably helps me feel better both about the child and about my ability to help. When we are free to choose whether we like children or not, the liking is cleaner, more honest.

It's harder when a parent doesn't seem to admire her children.

I've worked four years with Lukash's mother and she still won't praise her children's work. His 16 brothers and sisters don't greet him or say goodbye unless I tell them to. It amazes me that a family can survive at this nonverbal level. The only message I get from the mother about her children is that they should be good. If I knew anything else that would please her, I'd teach Lukash to do it, just to see her show some pride in him. She hasn't yet given me a clue as to what it might be. I've taught her children for four years, and still don't know what would get her excited about a child. Fortunately this problem is rare in so extreme a form. Despite Mama's inability to help, Lukash is making the class serve him. He's wise, having been around the prekindergarten longer than the other children. For two years he came with Mama to pick up Letty and Laura, and always watched what was going on with wide eyes, hiding behind Mama's skirt. We'd always greet him, but he never, ever answered us. Anyhow, being an old hand, he knows some special stuff. So, because he'd seen it in use last year, he got us to take out the water table in September, a bit earlier than usual. He also asked, pointing, for hula hoops, and was very funny with them, throwing the hoop so hard around his skinny hips that it circled him once or twice before it plopped to earth.

Nowadays when Mama comes to get Lukash, she brings Lucille with her. Lucille hides behind Mama and won't say "Hi" to me. She is just where Lukash was a year ago, Letty three years ago, and Laura before that. All year we will entice Lucille to peek out from Mama's skirts and see what school is about, and we will say "Hi" to her. In June we'll lend Mama a tricycle for Lucille to ride during the summer, since teaching that family to ride, first three-wheelers and then two-wheelers, has taken much of Katherine's energy over the years. By next year we hope Lucille will feel less strange with us.

By his fourteenth day of school Lukash, who never used to talk to me at all, walked right up to me in the morning and said, "Hi, Sydney!" and then grinned as I gasped, "Oh Lukash, good morning!" Then he turned on his heel and walked into HIS school.

3

Enough praise to go around: Positive reinforcement

"All right, then, I'll give him a balloon. I've got one left from my party. I'll go and get it now, shall I?"
"That, Piglet, is a very good idea. It is just what Eeyore wants to cheer him up. Nobody can be uncheered with a balloon."

—*Winnie-the-Pooh*

At the first birthday party of the year there's always a group of children who can't share the balloons. My balloon, they weep, my balloon, they clutch. Mine, mine, Kathye hugs a red one, sitting down, unwilling to play with it for fear of losing it. We encourage those who can to volley the balloons up into the air and play merrily with them. We quietly remind those clutching a balloon that it's more fun to play than to hold tight. As the year goes along, and there are more parties on more birthdays, and the weeping and clutching doesn't pay off at all, there finally comes a birthday when nobody cries, when all participate, when even Kathye has come to believe that sharing with the other kids is fun. This is one of the days when I'm exceedingly glad I teach.

A giggle: on Paulie's birthday he was shy and quiet. When Katherine asked him how it felt to be four, he responded, "Even better than three!"

The day Bev began school we noticed that she raced through tasks, seeming to experience neither pleasure nor success. So the next day, when she was speeding, this time with a parquetry toy, I complimented Amanda, across the table: "I really like how you go slow and careful when you're working, Amanda." Bev, who had been calling "look, teacher, look!" frequently during her race to nowhere, noted my praise of Amanda with some interest. Now again she called for attention. I just grunted "uhhuh" and turned my interest to someone else working steadily. By the end of the week Bev had paced herself more suitably, and we had said nothing against rushing. This is the gentlest way to use positive reinforcement. With any luck at all Bev will next come to notice how some techniques work better than others. Then accomplishing the task will become more important than pleasing us.

17

On her first day at school, Kathye cried as she looked at the flower by the door, and again when her mother left, though most children are ready to let go and easily give parents a goodbye hug. I suggested that Amanda sit close to Kathye to comfort her, and Amanda did, willingly. They watched us greet the others, saw parents leave, and heard us showing children their cubbies. It took weeks for Kathye to give up crying in the mornings, to believe that she was okay at school, so far away from her mother and the babies. One morning in October we logged that she cried instead of going to the toilet; cried instead of asking for a piece of watermelon; and cried rather than ask for a bike. Our strategy in the face of this crying is to give things to children who ask for them, letting Kathye figure out that asking works better. Watching the children really taught her that lesson, as she'd never have believed it from adults.

Our twins, Deena and Dinah, are very competitive, so we try to keep them apart. At the same time they are a great comfort to each other, so we don't try too hard. They were the first to learn to run and hug fallen children on the playground—logged in early October—just after Katherine had begun teaching it. One day they foiled our efforts to keep them apart and carried their rivalry into stringing beads. As they argued about whose was longer and whose was prettier, Katherine joined them and told first Dinah, then Deena, "Yours is very pretty"; "Yours is getting so long"; "I like how long yours is getting." When each one had enough praise they stopped fussing.

As the children gather for a meeting, I look for one who is sitting nicely, and say, "I like the way Millie came to the meeting." Then four more get ready, alert, wanting me to recognize them. So I do, and if I have to say it as many times as there are children, that's all right. I feel it's worth the time to give each one personal recognition for being ready for the meeting and behaving well.

By contrast, there's the experience of Johnny, home from his first day of first grade, whose mother asked him what it was like. He answered: "Sometimes she calls me 'class', and sometimes she calls me 'boys' and sometimes she calls me 'row four.' "

The most respectful way for a teacher to respond to children's feelings is by saying what she or he feels in response. These messages generally start with the word "I."

I think you're angry with Leslie.
I'm worried when you climb without holding on.
I want you to come here.
I think you can finish that.
I want to help.
I can teach you how to do it.
What do you want me to do?
I want you to remember our rule about hitting.
I need you to wait a minute.

Instead, we often see teachers whose whole attention is on behavior they say they don't like. When Kelly hits Janice, Mrs. Morgan yells and punishes Kelly first, only later comforting Janice. Our way is to put all the emphasis on the victim, saying "I'm so sorry you were hurt," and let the assailant stew in his or her own juice until the other poor little thing is feeling better. If the aggressor wants me, I say "Don't bother me. Can't you see I'm taking care of a hurt child?" While it is true that the violent child is in pain, I choose to attend to that pain later, after the hurt she or he has inflicted has been acknowledged and soothed.

At the beginning of each year teachers often find that we're working with children who persist in error in order to command attention. Parents who don't praise enough are thus compelled to attend to their children, and the children learn to control by being "bad" or "stupid."

Abby was really hungry for adult attention. Her family was disorganized in the clinical sense (see Eleanor Pavenstedt, *The Drifters*). She was obese, much larger than the other children. Despite her anxiety and fat, she had many appealing traits: it was Abby who showed visitors around the school, and helped care for smaller children. But little mother Abby didn't hold onto information very well. She had the adults stumped: we were unable to teach her something so she would still know it in a day or two. We were patient and kind to Abby, and tried many techniques, but the more attention we paid to her errors the more like a sieve she behaved. It finally occurred to me that we really couldn't take responsibility for Abby's learning; we had to get her to do that. We had been wrong to pay attention to her errors.

She liked to write, so I told her at her next writing lesson, "I'll stay right here with you as long as you make g's that look like g's. When you make a mistake, I'll leave."

She kept me there about three minutes, a record, and then erred. I left, wordlessly. The next day I went on with my experiment, and she worked even longer. This transferred to other activities, and became our way with Abby.

In September when I take out the camera, Lucretia zooms over and stands in front of the lens, making a frozen smile and other faces and saying "cheese." As I wander away from her toward those who are still working, I murmur, "I like to take pictures of children who are doing things." By the end of October, when she sees the camera she settles deeper into what she's doing, confident that she'll get to see a fine picture of herself at work.

Books of these photos are shelved with the commercial books and available to the children to enjoy. They get wonderfully dog-eared, fingermarked, and tattered if they aren't put into plastic photo holders.

To avoid making the child hate a difficult subject, you need to pay attention to his or her energy level and response and to sense when pressure will be productive. To pressure a child when you feel that discovery or understanding is near is to risk losing the child's tenuous connection with the subject matter. Yet there are times when a child makes no attempt, and misses the available triumph if we don't say, "Stretch! reach! you can get it if you just reach out!"

In a group of children, if there's one who understands and accepts your direction, you can praise that one and the others will come along, eager to do what you ask, wanting praise too. If you praise only what you admire, you can sidestep the danger that your praise may come to sound automatic. One can always find something to praise: good work, or graceful, humorous, or thoughtful acts.

When I want to get Kathye to sing alone, or to use a new language pattern, or anything else that takes courage, I first ask somebody who is secure, and then ask Kathye. Given a chance to observe, she sees that the activity is safe, and moves into it with less anxiety.

Sandy needs to be rocked; you know it, you can feel it. She's having trouble at home, or a big frustration just happened. Her body is tense, her face babyish, her shoulders tight. You want to rock Sandy, she'd enjoy it, but you don't want to single her out and add to the troubles she's already carrying. So you look for somebody in good shape, someone like Marcus, who is just *fine*. You sit in the rocker and call, "Marcus, come sit in my lap for a little." And you rock Marcus and croon to him and a little line forms. Now either Sandy is in line, and you rock her, or she's not, and you say, "Sandy, I want to rock you too. I'll let you know when it's your turn."

Many practices common in schools damage and belittle children. There's the obvious, nasty sort, where big people tell little ones that they're "animals" or "stupid" or "clumsy." A subtle, twisted sort insinuates that the child is likely to cheat, lie, or behave badly if you, the powerful teacher, don't keep constant vigilance. A case in point is the widespread practice of disregarding a sea of raised hands to search out and shame the child who doesn't know the answer. Fear may keep children alert, but it won't teach them love of learning.

John Holt (see Bibliography I) says that it's belittling to ask anyone a question whose factual answer you already know. Teachers are forever doing this, even though it's unnatural and disrespectful. So, instead of testing all the time, and disapproving of the wrong answers, we try to use the form, "Do you know what color this is?" or "Please tell me what color this is," or "Please count these blocks," or "What color do you see here?" rather than "What color is this?" or "How many blocks are there?" as if we didn't know. This way our functions are kept clear: your learning belongs to you, and if you will trust me with information about what you've already learned, I can then go on to help you learn some more.

A different kind of misguidance appears in questions like: "Do you want to wash up now?" or "How would you like to rest now?" These are commands cloaked in question form, and the teacher who puts the questions is not listening for answers. Better to be clear and direct: "Time to clean up now." Or, "I want you to do such-and-such."

What constitutes a proper reward for a child at school? Surely nothing tangible, nothing extrinsic. Our colleague Amy Williams, a prekindergarten social worker, got really excited about the reading program at Burnett and the general level of diversity, discipline, and response in our class. She told us that her son had been in a Montessori school for more than two years without learning to read. She finally sat down with a roll of pennies and told him, "You are going to read." He learned, of course. "But I wouldn't do it that way now," she said. "I much prefer the way these children learn, with only smiles, hurrahs, and clapping from the grownups."

Similarly, the only food rewards that make sense to me are those that taste good and build health. We offer pineapple, sunflower seeds, and other fruit as treats. But we never say, "If you learn this you can have some pineapple." To reward the children for serious effort and wit, we hang their work on the classroom walls. This sense of the school as an exhibition hall dictates careful spacing, lighting, and mounting of each work of art, and since all the children are gifted we exhibit something made by each child. Space is limited, so just about all the work we exhibit is made entirely by children. Their silhouettes, made when we trace their shadows on black paper, are exceptions to the rule, as are materials from the cultures of the children's families, but these, too, reflect that the room is the children's place.

We've learned to deal with the realities of vandalism, so when we hang our children's fine work in corridors where work may be destroyed, we add some fringe or other geegaws to the framing, to attract the vandals away from the children's work. We display children's drawing, painting, and collage, and sometimes math work, stories they've dictated, sewing, clay work, group murals, and photographs of them at their activities.

I don't believe in rewarding hard work with play. I like to mix up play and work at school, since I believe that adults at our best times have no greater pleasure than doing good work, while at our worst we get no joy from what we call play. When Daphne has done some math very well, her reward is an offer of more arithmetic. When Lucretia has completed a puzzle she may choose to repeat that puzzle or do the next harder one. We ask: "Would you like a harder puzzle, since you did that one so well?" When children have been seated for some time, we offer climbing or dancing next. This doesn't reward sitting still but trains them to relieve physical fatigue by using the body variously.

One reward teachers use is the celebration of holidays. Making sure they're a pleasure isn't easy, since interrupting the routine can disturb little children. A good teacher uses holidays to reinforce the goals of the program. A poor teacher, preoccupied with pumpkins, turkeys, bunnies and paper chains, loses touch with the children's needs. It doesn't serve children to cut and color paper sym-

bols for the holidays. Those traditional symbols were always made by children
to please grownups. Artist Edwin Cerney, a gifted teacher, was amazed one
April to find Native American children assigned to draw Easter bunnies. He
encouraged their teachers to abandon the bunnies, and allow the children to
bring out the wonderful drawings of horses from where they were hidden in their
desks.

Children's and parents' styles dominate any celebration. Before Hallowe'en
we tell the parents that they may send the children to school in costumes, but we
don't permit masks at school. This rule comes from repeated experience with
threes and young fours who are terrified by masked children. They may spend
hours getting over the fright even after it has been demystified. School is too
new, and our story that school is safe is too untried, for us to allow masks in
October.

Daphne came to school in face make-up and a plastic store-bought costume,
already uncomfortable first thing in the morning. I told her to feel free to take off
any parts she wanted off, and as the day proceeded she removed her costume,
piece by piece, and rubbed off the make-up.

Bev arrived in make-up, a wig, a hat, her pants rolled to different heights,
and an extra jacket over her sweater. She appeared a beautiful, exciting clown.
Her mother has an eye for all things dramatic. She enjoyed being dressed up all
day, in contrast to Daphne's discomfort. None of the other children was in
costume. Some of them knew why Daphne and Bev were dressed up, others
needed explanations. Lucretia worried all day; a Jehovah's Witness, she had
never heard of Hallowe'en, and expressed concern: "Dose little girls don't
spozed to wear make-up." When we dressed up the others in clothes from our
dollhouse so they could be part of Hallowe'en too, Lucretia declined.

Lukash went to dress up, but scurried back to Katherine to complain: "Don-
cha got no boy stuff?" We should have expected this, since his father never let
the girls come to school in pants. Katherine showed him the jackets and firehats
and trousers and big men's dress shoes, and he had a fine time dressing up.
Lamar, whose people have no such regulations, put on a white party dress and a
blue hat with veil; later he changed into a blue velvet dress. Everybody got
dressed up except Lucretia, yet the crazy, out-of-hand energy that mars most
children's Hallowe'ens·was missing from ours. Aside from admiring and photo-
graphing the children in costume, our morning routines went as usual, through
work period and snack. After snack, Katherine and I each gathered a group of
kids, a knife, and a pumpkin. Everybody helped carve and smell and taste the
pumpkin. When we lit it with a candle the room grew quiet and the children's
eyes grew big as they marveled at our jack-o'lanterns. Next we went over to the
rug, where there were tubs of water for bobbing for apples. The first bobber
was Dinah, who—unable to get the apple instantly—concluded "I can't." I
countered, "Oh, sure you can," and she got it next time. In fact, everybody got

an apple without using hands, and the children enjoyed seeing that Katherine and I had the same kinds of troubles they had.

At dismissal Amanda's mother was glad to take our pumpkin seeds home, bake them, and send them back to school next day. Eating pumpkin seeds is a Black American tradition, and it made Amanda feel good to bring us a treat.

Our Hallowe'en had four parts: the regular, routine start of the day; the small groups cutting the pumpkins; taking turns in the circle bobbing for apples; and dressing up and being admired, with much looking in the full-length mirrors. The day rewarded the children with modest pleasures.

Traditional rewards were things like sitting near the teacher or getting gold stars. In a modern child-centered classroom, neither teacher nor child has a particular location, since where you work depends on what you're doing. We get gummed stars in all colors and put them on things for prettiness. Instead of using them to reward children, we let the praise itself ring out in the room for all work done well.

4

Everybody's an exception: Recognizing children's styles

"Tigger is all right really," said Piglet lazily.

"Of course he is," said Christopher Robin.

"Everybody is really," said Pooh. "That's what I think," said Pooh. "But I don't suppose I'm right," he said.

"Of course you are," said Christopher Robin.

—The House at Pooh Corner

"Well," said Owl, "the fact is," he said, "I don't know what they're like," said Owl frankly.

—The House at Pooh Corner

Two children rarely do anything the same way. Most writing for teachers is misleading because it talks about "the child" as if there were only one. We are given little help in the large task of differentiating one child's ways and means from another's. If our planning is to work it must work for real children, the one who pushes while making fruit salad, the one who's scared of dogs, and the one who needs privacy to try new things.

While I could teach most children the Meeting Song using my best group technique, Dinah seemed to make no attempt to learn it. It appeared that she had decided not to bother. Dissatisfied, I tried something else. That night I asked my son Alex, a fine singer, to record the song on a cassette. He sang it through several times. When I gave the tape to Dinah she chose to hear it five times, and those twenty or so renditions taught her the song, which she sang in a big voice at the meeting that day, proudly and with dignity:

There's a meeting here tonight
There's a meeting here tonight
I know you by your friendly face
There's a meeting here tonight.

What this tells us is that Dinah doesn't want to be out in public while learning; she likes to be seen only when she has something put together. If we remember

24

this we'll be better able to teach Dinah other things. Too often, in too many classrooms, Dinah is ignored or flunked. However, if we pay close attention to her style, she too can experience success. Good teaching implies being comfortable making exceptions for people when they need them. It is the opposite of that killer phrase my teachers used to use: "If I do it for you, I'll have to do it for everybody." This was untrue and unfair. We never treat two people alike, and most people don't mind exceptions being made in exceptional circumstances.

Children use a given material to explore different visions of their own. Take, for example, our miniature dollhouse furniture. We have some streamlined Danish chairs, sofas, kitchen appliances, all of wood, some little enamelled toilets and sinks and bathtubs, and many many tacky plastic tables, chairs, beds, and TVs. There are tiny dollies to scale. We keep all this in a tub with some carpet samples, near empty shelves that can be used for one-, two- and three-story houses.

Daphne chooses this material regularly, apparently working on issues of spatial and personal relationship. We see her putting dolls in the rooms she makes, sometimes putting Mama and child on a sofa or bed; and often putting folks in the bathroom.

Lukash took out the dollhouse furniture and built it all up as if it were blocks, into one skyscraper with the bathtub on the very top, and two dolls in the bathtub! My first reaction was to say, "Lukash, that's not the way you're supposed to use the furniture." I stifled that and said instead, "Lukash, don't take it down till Katherine has seen it." Then, discharging my need for order, I said "You used the furniture as if it were blocks." I sent Lukash to Katherine, knowing that he would be praised and see his wit reflected in her eyes.

Our twins are teaching us a lot about support systems. First Deena helped her sister to some food at snack time. Then there were many, many occasions when Dinah came around, asking where her sister was, or what she was doing. On at least one occasion, when I asked Dinah what she wanted to do, she said "I want to be where my sister is."

I like to teach children to stand on their heads because it's a change of perspective, an achievement, and something I myself am afraid to try. Most kids just trust me and hop up on their heads with a little help. Some don't trust easily. I remember trying to teach Marie. I said, "Come here, Marie. I want to teach you how to stand on your head." She looked right at me and said, "I don't know how to stand on my head." So I smiled reassuringly and said, "That's all right, but come here and I'll *teach* you how." I showed her other children who'd just learned how. Marie was so sure she couldn't do it that it took the whole force of my personality to win her over. I showed her how it works safely, because we work alongside the wall and I stay right there to rescue children with problems. Emily Beals-Nesmith, who used to teach at Burnett, says to children in such situations, "I don't ask you to do things that are too hard for you." When

Marie's mother came to get her that day, she brought her over to the spot where we practice headstands, and showed her how she *could*! Three months later, Marie and my daughter Jenny were the two children who could do headstands in the middle of the room, away from the supporting wall. In fact, they were the only two children who still chose to do headstands at all.

Some children arrive at prekindergarten with no sense at all of their separateness. They've been their mothers' dollies, kept passive and quiet. Adults make all their decisions. It's distressing to see a child of four whose response to anything new is to wait. Frequently they even look like dolls, arriving in dressy clothing rather than the work clothes we suggest at the intake interview. Such children need to be left alone while the teacher is conspicuously busy with others who are making demands and choices. Given adults who respond immediately and warmly to even hesitant demands, they learn fast to be real children.

I learned from Lissa Mattross to cut up green paper and make it available as play money. Deena and Amanda collected it all and put it in purses. This was the basic game until Leslie adopted the money. She used it first in the block area, and later in the schoolyard and on the dome. The other children were less possessive about it, but some days there was a store where Lukash sold toys to those who came with money. Things would cost one or two, no unit specified and no change given. Lukash liked collecting all that money, but he didn't like having the game end. He'd give some money back to kids who were broke, so they'd come and shop some more.

By year's end, the money had been used so much that I had to throw it away and make up a fresh supply!

5

Values:
Independence, interdependence,
and cooperation

"That's right," said Eeyore. "Sing. Umty-tiddly, umty-too. Here we go gathering Nuts and May. Enjoy yourself."
"I am," said Pooh.

—Winnie-the-Pooh

When I want them to gather together, I try to give the children some notice: "In five minutes we're going to have a meeting." They don't know what five minutes is, but it's a way of saying, "I respect what you're doing and want to give you time to finish it before I take over."

Since Katherine and I coordinate our work, the children needn't always move together. If some children eat quickly and others take longer, Katherine helps the fast eaters get back to work while I sit with the others. I've visited preschool classes where as much as one-third of the children's time was spent waiting: waiting on line for breakfast, waiting to wash hands, waiting for crayons to be passed out, waiting for a grownup to take you to the toilet, waiting to go out-doors, waiting on line for a drink. We move as one only for some intrinsic reason; otherwise individual rhythms prevail. When Leslie needs me but I'm going to be busy with Lukash for a while, I help her make a plan for that time, or find someone else to help her. The children feel our respect for their time, and on the rare occasions when they have to wait they do so with a fair amount of grace.

When thinking about issues of dependence and cooperation, it helps to keep your priorities clear, and to regularly question your routines to see it they benefit children and bring a cooperative world closer.

The children are painfully aware of their dependence on our decisions. It is most debilitating for them to have to sit and wait. Look at children in doctors' waiting rooms and in clothing stores where they must simply tag along and stay out from underfoot. At school we try to have the time, like the chairs, fit the children.

When gathering a group we tell the children what to do if they get there early, so they won't have to waste their time waiting. If we're meeting at the rug, they're supposed to look at a book; thus the bookcase is near the rug. When everybody has arrived, I call them by name to return their books to the shelves, praising those who handle them carefully and reshelve them well.

We try to be aware when skills have been integrated. As the year progresses and the children become accustomed to shelving their books, we ask children to call on others to return their books. We encourage these monitors to praise good work, and we give them language for correcting errors: "Please put it away carefully", or "Be careful with our books."

All of these procedures help the children escape dependency on us, and let the school belong more directly to them.

The children come to me when their business is really with each other:

"Sydney, Jason's messing with me." "How do you feel when Jason messes with you?" "I don't like it." "Go tell Jason 'I don't like it when you mess with me.' "

"Sydney, Irwin won't share the Lego." "How do you feel when he leaves you out?" "It makes me mad." "Tell Irwin you're mad because he won't share."

"Sydney, I wanna go up in the tree house and there's already two in it." "Good counting. Talk to the kids up there and tell them you're waiting."

"Sydney, Susan didn't put her glass away after snack." "Do you want to put it away for her, or are you going to tell her she forgot?"

"Sydney, tie my shoe." "Ask Nicole to tie it for you. She ties them well nowadays."

"Sydney, I can't unbutton my coat." "See if Maurice wants to help you. He has strong fingers."

The children are enormously competent. They can help each other in many, many ways. But they seldom see the forest of each other for the dominant presence of our adult trees. At home few relatives regularly remember to send children to help each other. At school we can, and do. From the log:

Donnie has started telling Katherine what to do: "You should take your Lego apart, too. Don't tie Sandy's shoe, neither, a kid can do it. Put tape here, too, Katherine." Also he's keeping track of the children who are absent, and "Willie wasn't here yesterday, neither."

Other cultures handle issues of interdependency differently. From a slide show I once saw about childcare in China, two images stay with me. The first was a single string stretched between two children, each of whom threaded beads from one end to the middle, which rested on the table. I've adopted this activity, and now offer both partner and solitaire bead-stringing. Second, the Chinese make children's shirts that button up the back, so that by going to others for help with their buttons children learn to function collectively.

In the light of this information I examined my own practices, and found myself of at least two minds. Cooperation, yes, I said to myself (and all my friends.) Dependency, no. I had always taught kids to put their coats on by laying them (button side up) on the floor, standing at the collar end, putting hands deep into the armholes, and throwing the coats over their heads. But this was not intended to keep them away from each other; it was to keep their parents from dressing them. When I lived in New York where children wore heavy winter clothing, they put on their coats this way, then helped each other with buttons and belts and boots. It felt at once intimate and independent.

6

Plain food and fancy theory:
On eating in the classroom

Pooh always liked a little something at eleven o'clock in the morning, and he was very glad to see Rabbit getting out the plates and mugs; and when Rabbit said, "Honey or condensed milk with your bread?" he was so excited that he said, "Both," and then, so as not to seem greedy, he added, "But don't bother about the bread, please."

—Winnie-the-Pooh

The conventional wisdom about eating in the early childhood classroom went like this: use the food as a device for socialization; exploit children's natural interest in eating, and introduce names, categories, and labels while food makes them receptive; vary the sorts of cookies by shape and teach shapes, etc.

Well, I don't.

I think that food we provide should be nourishing (not cookies in our overweight culture), attractive, and eaten in a tranquil environment. I don't enjoy dining with messy fours and fives, nor eating the bland fare children love. One task I won't do for parents is teach table manners. Aren't they arbitrary anyway? And the old-fashioned system of the group sitting down to a snack or a meal wastes valuable work time. Besides, people get hungry at different times and we want children to recognize when they're hungry or thirsty without our telling them. So that's the case against the classic sitdown meal with children.

We prefer buffet-style service that is available as long as possible, always considering the staff, who need to prepare the food and to clean up afterwards. We let the children decide when, how much and for how long they will eat. Their eating styles and degrees of independence can be very informative to us if we watch their behavior rather than making them do it our way. Since we're in California we can often eat outdoors, so we take finger foods with us when we go out to play. Outdoors, children often eat food they've snubbed indoors.

To make this casual eating work, children need three routines. They must know how to take only the amount they're sure they'll eat, how to put it on a plate and take it to a sitting place, and how to dispose of their dirty dishes and

30

napkin. Normal fours learn this in the first six weeks of school, and then it's an unhurried, graceful activity to watch.

Children have a big investment in food. They feel they know what they're doing when they're eating. We try to build on this, especially with those who haven't much confidence in other areas. They're impressed when we let them pour their own milk from a container or pitcher. When Amanda spills milk, early in the year, everyone looks worried, watching closely as I explain where the sponge is, so she can clean up the mess. At the start of each year such incidents test our ability to show them that school will be fair, demanding, and fun.

The first days have important implications for the whole year. If Leslie takes food, tastes it, and decides she doesn't want it, she needn't finish it since she made the attempt. But if her glass has a lot of milk in it, she must drink it, because that's the amount she chose for herself. It's not okay when Deena puts a sandwich on Dinah's plate, so Katherine tells her to take it back. We work on independent eating, hoping that the American tendency to overweight can be offset by children who have learned to figure out what they want to eat. Children learn that we realize they're no longer babies.

There's less fuss at school than at home about what the children eat. Our goal is for each child to notice what she or he wants and how much, then to take that much and eat it. We don't make food demands often; when we do, we ask them to eat one bite of zucchini or other unusual food, to learn what it is.

Many four-year-olds have no idea whether they want a little or a lot. Those up against competition for food at home are especially poor judges of what they really want. We try hard to have enough food to satisfy each child. Lukash, with 14 older and two younger rival siblings, stuffs in everything he can get as fast as possible, then chomps on it for a long time. We're encouraging him to try another way, hoping that if we pile food on his plate he will trust us enough to take the smaller bites we recommend. We suppose he's been doing what he must to survive, but in this different environment we want him to learn that he can relax while eating.

We take all portable leftovers out to the play yard, where Deena, for one, continues to nibble although she was full indoors.

I saw Amanda scraping the white out of her apple with her teeth. I said I thought her teeth were sharp enough to bite through the skin. She tried. They were, and she ate the whole apple. Next week I saw her scraping the white out with her teeth again. I repeated about her sharp teeth. Again she obediently ate it up. It will probably take a few more times before she either decides to eat apples with the skin on, or tells me that she hates skin and doesn't want to eat it any more. I'd be as pleased with the assertiveness as with the other outcome.

One year we were able to control our school menu. The only canned foods we served were tuna fish and frozen orange juice. Meats were fresh, without preservatives. Fruits and vegetables were fresh and in season. We had a simple, repetitious menu, one that children like and will eat. On Mondays we had peanut butter sandwiches, on Tuesdays eggs, on Wednesdays we had tuna sandwiches, on Thursday our favorite, chicken, and on Friday we had spaghetti with meat sauce or hamburgers. I hope that nutrition-conscious teachers will press for this kind of clean food in school.

Another innovation was giving the children a drink with nutritional (not baking) yeast in it once a week. They resisted it a little at first, although the frozen orange juice concentrate makes it tasty. By year's end, most requested seconds of our Smoothie, and by then we made it twice a week.

Many teachers do a lot of cooking with young children. I have trouble with that because so much of what they cook is high in sugar or sodium or both. I won't make jello for anybody, least of all young children. We do make fruit salad and pop corn. I like to bring in a whole ripe sunflower, take it apart and eat it with the children.

I heard a preschool teacher asking the children what they ate for breakfast. Somebody named one of those awful sugared cereals. The teacher attacked: "Doesn't your mama know better? You tell her you want some cooked cereal." I think it's a terrible mistake to tell a little child that his mama is raising him wrong. A teacher's hostility can threaten the child's respect for his mother, the teacher, or both. It becomes school against home, defeating mutual communication and trust. If the teacher is serious, she has access to the parent, and can respectfully report what she's learned about nutrition. I believe that if the teacher knew that the parent was also her employer, this kind of abuse would be curbed.

7

"They doan whup you if you say it's a accident" The bedwetters group

Pooh explained to Eeyore that Tigger was a great friend of Christopher Robin's, who had come to stay in the Forest, and Piglet explained to Tigger that he mustn't mind what Eeyore said because he was always gloomy; and Eeyore explained to Piglet that, on the contrary, he was feeling particularly cheerful this morning; and Tigger explained to anybody who was listening that he hadn't had any breakfast yet.

—*The House at Pooh Corner*

Another area in which fours are expert is toilet training. The fours in prekindergarten are all dry during the day except for occasional accidents, but some still wet at night. We identified five bedwetters in the class the year Delfina Sabogal served an internship at Burnett, working toward her Ph.D. in psychology. We met once a week with the five children, helping them express their feelings about themselves as people who wet the bed. We knew about some of them from the intake interview, and others from the way they smelled some mornings or from their conversation.

Delfina prepared for the group meeting by pouring a cup of water on the rug, and putting a doll on it. Then she invited the children to the rug, and asked about the doll. "Why did the baby wet the bed?" As soon as Jeffrey knew what was going on, he covered his eyes with his hands. Others in the group were matter-of-fact, and explained to us that "babies is 'posta wet the bed, but kids ain't", and that "a dream makes you wet the bed." They gave each other good advice, much as adults, sitting around smoking, give each other pointers on how to stop.

Jeffrey handled the second session quietly, but wasn't forthcoming about the reasons the kid (this time an "older" teddy bear) had wet his bed. Other children revealed some of their strategies to us. One sleeps in her mother's bed and wets because she's mad at her mother. Another reports, "They doan whup you if you say it's a accident." At the third meeting of the group, Delfina again asked, "Why did the kid wet the bed?" Jeffrey blurted, "It's dark in the hall and it's too far to the bathroom." When we suggested a night light to Jeffrey's mother she was willing to try one. She was also eager to pour out many of her childrearing troubles, and Delfina made herself available to counsel with her.

We set out to discover why the five held on to a behavior that made them wet and smelly and ashamed. There were differing answers in different families, but we all felt better for having aired the subject. The parents approved, feeling less isolated and desperate when they knew that we considered the problem worth our attention. If only every classroom teacher could learn to do group work from someone like Delfina! And had an associate like Katherine to keep the others safe and productive during group time!

Incidentally, I don't think parents teach children to be toilet trained. I think parents make it clear that they'd like waste products deposited in a particular place. And when the children are ready to cooperate with the parents, they toilet train themselves. All children end up toilet trained—those whose parents make a big deal of it and those whose parents make no fuss at all.

8

"Ivan the terrible":
Sheltering the out-of-bounds child

"It's Christopher Robin," he said.
"Ah, then you'll be all right," said Piglet. "You'll be quite safe with him. Good-
bye," and he trotted off home as quickly as he could, very glad to be Out of All
Danger again.

—Winnie-the-Pooh

The strongest child I've ever encountered was Ivan. He had gone to a foster home in July of his fourth year when his parents abandoned him, his two older sisters and his baby brother. By August he'd been seen by a doctor, diagnosed as hyperactive, and put on Ritalin until his foster mother decided to take him off medication. I'm glad she took him off, because I don't want to work with drugged children. The one time I was asked to work with a child on Ritalin, I agreed to do so only if he was freed from medication. The loving gardener cultivates without chemicals. When children need to find self-control, let's spare them from dependence on drugs. (See Peter Schrag's book, listed in Bibliography 1.)

In September Ivan came to our class. Here are our log entries about him:

September 15. Anxious that I take his picture in a hurry! Rode bike strongly. Heard story tape twice; later told his foster mother, "It says, 'Turn the page, the cow jump over the moon.'" Turns pages well. Loved organ, but turned the switch on and off despite our telling him to leave the switch alone. Went up the treehouse. A bee came by him in the playground and he freaked out, terrified. Very excited when he eats: dropped food on the floor three times. Eats largely.

September 16. Played a lot of organ, ate a lot again. Pulled Georgia in the wagon. Heard a tape a couple of times. Asked Katherine if he could help her put out the bikes again, and did it with good sense, returning for another bike after each one was out without any adult prompting.

September 17. Enjoyed story, *Caps for Sale*—he'd heard it before, some-where. Can restrain himself from talking out of turn, but it's really hard for him, since what he has to say is so powerful. Said his sisters and brother and mother hate him.

September 20. Put bikes away on his own. Likes responsibility. Planted a marigold. Up the ladder. Worked a long time on a collective drawing: made a person who later became a monster. Decided to let cottage cheese slop down his chin when his mouth was full. Very messy. This bothered Katherine who told him not to do it, and he stopped.

September 21. Got weary toward end of day but couldn't talk about his fatigue and its cause with me. Tested well on verbal, visual, and number—is classically bright. On the phone in the playhouse, talking to Joyce, whom he calls "my girlfriend." Told Katherine, "She doesn't like me, she loves me." He began reading, and his first two words were "Ivan" and "teacher." Painted— his original picture disappears under a second layer each time he paints.

September 22. Wanted to remember his reading words by their sequence, but learned how to identify them by their appearance, instead.

September 24. The others are upset by his boisterous interruptions of our meetings. Ivan needs to be helped to be calm in the group. We'll try having Katherine sit close so we don't need to interrupt the meeting just because he does. Asked for his mother's name to read. Says she misses him too. Picks up everything fast—body language as well as verbal. Someday this will be a safe space for Ivan.

September 27. Very angry today, erupted and erupted. Settled for permission to go out in the yard and yell and run around. Strongest four-year-old I've ever known! Punched pillow. Volunteered to be rocked. I'm exhausted.

September 28. Conference is set up for next week with his Department of Social Services worker, his foster mother, and my friend, Dr. Martin Shaffer, a psychologist. I am feeling relief that we are getting to work on this child's problems, since his pain is apparent most of the time. His bedwetting is regular and made placement in a foster home hard; all four children wet the bed every night, from the eleven-year-old down to the baby.

October 1. Conference: hard to talk with foster mother since she was taking Ivan and Harry home, and "keeping" two other children, all of whom kept interrupting our conference.

She feels that he's too demanding and sometimes "gets to" her—she appears genteel, but pushed one of the little kids hard. Another person struggling to do her best, I take it. She said we could make a home visit.

October 6. Seemed to hold back when playing with our inflated swords with Rita. Very gentle. When playing Lotto Katherine had five boards and gave three to Ivan and two to Harry, promising Harry three next time. But Ivan said, generously, "Give it to Harry."

October 7. I read a story about a rocking chair, and then he asked, in a little boy voice (not his usual tough, sophisticated way at all), "Sydney, give me some lovin." Says his foster mother doesn't hold him on her lap. Said he likes his Daddy's lap.

October 11. Lots of hugging and "I love you" and asking for lap, loving. Does it in righteous fashion, asks and accepts in a way I can only admire. Certain it will come. Uses food for confrontation a lot—grabbed the pomegranate we were all sharing and licked it, very gross for the adults to deal with. Can't use machines for a week because he's still unwilling to leave on and off switches to the grownups. I love him, but he does get to me.

October 12. Absolutely plays dominoes—counts, knows colors, moves. Asked to join Harry and Moses and played nicely.

October 13. Doesn't do the bear puzzle as well as we'd expect. Is it because the baby bear is cuddled up to the mama?

October 19. Very negative day. Unplugged the projector which freaked Katherine out—ran out of the yard. Cried when I held and rocked him. I sent up flares to our social worker. Is barred from using the projector for a week.

October 20. Good day, perhaps because lots of rocking and loving early in the day, later a hug as he came to the meeting kept him in pretty good shape.

October 22. Phone rang early and he asked, "Should I get it?" I said, "No, thank you." This is Ivan letting me regulate his behavior! Let him have the projector back (told him his week was up—so I lied a little) and he loved seeing his slides again.

October 25. He found Anita bleeding and crying in the yard and *carried* her across the yard to Katherine!

November 4. Reluctant to do arts, wants to r-r-rum little cars all the time, but enjoys art when I tell him to paint or draw for a little while. Like kids who hate to get into or out of the bathtub.

November 15. Visited Ivan's home. It is visually very stimulating, many plants and many, many decorative objects around. Seven or eight children running in and out made me unable to attend to much of anything there. Ivan liked having me at his house, but seemed more concerned that the other kids shouldn't get next to me than with enjoying me himself.

My friend Isobel visiting today noticed that Ivan has a deep and fine feeling for poetry and music—gets out of himself and into the music and is whole. He delighted her when he chanted, at snack, "Yummy in the tummy."

November 22. Got in trouble twice—once he "messed with" my labelmaker and got benched, emerging contrite to a fine reading lesson. Other time he threw water at Nell, who cried and cried and cried until Ivan looked really ashamed.

November 23. Cursing a lot. Called me "bitch" and used all the big ones quietly to me; my line is that I don't mind those words but there are people who mind them and Ivan had better be careful how he uses them around those people. He knows that some of the children really don't like cursing, and that I support their insistence that he not hurt them this way.

Well behaved and a delight at the Ella Jenkins concert—shouted heartfelt responses to the mime who opened the concert: "We won't hurt you!" etc. Just peachy!

December 8. Told me about the time his mother asked him to get a knife when she was fighting, said, "I stayed in the bed." Who was she fighting? "My Daddy." Testing today included: riding bike indoors over the mat kids were tumbling on; piling toast on the table; climbing up a bookcase; and throwing raisins.

Curled up in a sunny spot with a book for a while. I called him my kitty and took another picture for him to enjoy in the slide projector.

December 9. Jealous when our social worker went off with another kid.

(After winter vacation we were less regular in our logging, since we felt we had a pretty good idea of who the children were.)

February 1. (Logged by Polly, student teacher) Sydney really "sat on" Ivan today. He really needed it. (Yea! Sydney.)

February 2. Told me "My heart is breaking." Turns out his sister kicked him in the stomach.

February 6. Gets a lot out of slugging the pillow. He sometimes yells at a particular person, sometimes feels his pain visibly. He remembers to ask for the pillow often, and is glad when we think to offer it to him.

February 7. Ivan's dream: I was in a hospital with my mother and she went home and I stole nine dollars from the bank and the police ran after me and I was dead.

February 8. Helped the sub run the class.

February 9. "Bad dreams come from your *stupid* brain." "I wanted my dream to *live!*"

February 14. Disturbed all morning after walk to park. Told Katherine "That's where Robert, my Mama's boyfriend, died; he set the house afire."

March 4. Asked if Richard, a visior, was Polly's husband. Also whispered delicately to me, "Can I give him a hug?"

Children in our room toilet themselves when they need to, eat when they're hungry, and paint when the spirit moves them. Ivan couldn't manage these freedoms without abusing them—hurting children and trashing their work—so we had to construct a safe place for him, inside the space the rest of the children use as a school. Sometimes this meant limiting his choices to activities he couldn't spoil for the others by being wild, so, for instance, we wouldn't let him build blocks with others.

Sometimes, usually late in the week, he could be treated more or less like the others, except that we had to check more often that he was okay. Otherwise we'd find that he had disrupted several children. When Ivan was really flailing about, incapable of self-control, I'd make him into an extension of my left hand. He'd go through the day with me, like a baby in a stroller, stopping when I stopped, going where I went, and being repeatedly exposed to situations where other children were praised for doing reasonable things.

Every day Ivan tested the strength of our rules. At the beginning of the year he tried us several hundred times a day. He'd crash his bike into other bikes, shove the dollhouse dishes off the table where a nice "party" was going on, and yell during the softest parts of a story I'd be reading. By the end of the year, on a good day, there'd be fewer than a dozen times when he'd test us.

He spent enormous energy determining that we were indeed strong enough to take care of him. I took the slide projector to be repaired each of the three times he threw it on the floor. He found that he got a fair amount of attention from me when he broke an expensive machine, so he repeated the behavior. Then he got stuck to my left hand for a number of days, unable to choose what he played with, the way the other children did. He got no direct attention from me in this way. I just tugged him to come along, and sat him down next to me wherever I sat. This way he saw the class from my perspective—children working steadily and checking with adults before they moved on to other work or play.

Since he'd always gotten attention at home for being "bad", he was already convinced when he reached school that survival means being bad enough to get all the attention you need. We had to let him know that people can have attention for being good, and that they can even have it for free! Reports from his kindergarten teacher next year showed that he'd largely learned this hard lesson.

We carefully heeded what Ivan told us, responded respectfully, and talked about him only with people we knew would help him. It became clear to him that with us he could safely express his pain.

Ivan confided some really horrible experiences to us. Once, when he was less than four, his mother and father were fighting and his mother told him to get her a knife. He reported that he didn't do it. To refuse complicity in violence is heroic at any age.

The other children don't involve themselves directly in the problems of an Ivan. They may have sympathy, but he disrupts the environment enough to make them very glad to see a grownup step in and firmly restore order. Disorder is frightening. Children can relax when a fair teacher is in charge. Healthy children naturally keep a little distance from neurotic ones. The healthy ones would like things to be better, but know that they haven't the power to control such a child. When they are getting what they need from the environment, they don't begrudge him special care.

Children need to know that they have strong people around them, and teachers have to be sensitive to the use and abuse of power. Adults owe children at least a few years of safety. Consequently I often feel even more put off by permissive, kindly, weak teachers than by authoritarian, strict, powerful ones. We all seek to feel the substance and power of our comrades and mentors, but little children need it by virtue of their powerlessness.

When children pretend to be Superman, Batman, Wonder Woman, or the Lone Ranger, what they're saying about themselves is, "The only way to be safe is to have a powerful ally, and this character will be mine, and protect me." A child with a toy gun is making the same statement.

Can't we do more for children than give them fantasy characters and toy guns? Guns are banned in our classroom. The children must at least once in their lives meet people who say you can't shoot your way out of your troubles.

Grownups a child can count on may supply a breathing space in a hard world for benign fantasy, delight, joy, and ecstasy, by shielding children as much as possible from what is harsh, cruel, thoughtless and immoral. The worst damaged children *require* this kind of fence around their pasture. They need to know we will take care of them when they're angry—even when they are angry at us.

Ivan could trust us to take over when his self-control gave out. He acknowledged his feelings and expressed them, expecting us to be the grownups and keep him safe. We were proud when we could.

In a year when others read an average of thirty words by June, Ivan read ninety. He was brilliant, absorbing at a fierce rate all the material we gave him. We made him books on all his important subjects: who he loved, what frightened him, staying dry at night, riding the two-wheeler. He learned to use this wonderful reading to take charge of some of his out-of-control life. However, his real brilliance lay in being clearer about what he was feeling than most adults ever become. And he demanded solutions to his very real, though sometimes insoluble, problems. We couldn't make his parents want Ivan. We couldn't make his sisters be kind to him. As a child who had been through violent and painful experiences all his four years, Ivan had ample excuse to become squashed, a vegetable. Instead, his vitality was deeply attractive, and his contact with his inner states nothing less than inspired. Every year, when we discuss skin color, some children tell me I'm black like them. Ivan was one of these. I'm pleased if they see me as black, because that's the color of the people they love. (I have straight, dark hair, brown eyes, and very pale skin. Only someone who was black and loved me and was projecting could think I was black.) I tell the children I'm glad they love me. And I tell them I'm white. It seems important to me that they hear that someone they care for happens to be white. It was hard for Ivan to hear me say this. I'm not sure he ever really accepted my story. If he didn't, I'm glad to be black for Ivan.

Perspective

An accidental teacher

". . . Kanga was fidgeting about and saying, "Just one more jump, dear, and then we must go home."

—*Winnie-the-Pooh*

In 1962, when teachers were in great demand, I became a teacher almost by accident. I was never trained as a teacher, and I didn't do student teaching. I came in the back door. My undergraduate courses in history, psychology and anthropology qualified as courses in the education department, so I was eligible for an emergency teaching credential. At the time I knew nothing about teaching except that I wanted to teach better than I'd been taught, and, as a free spirit, I didn't want to teach what others told me to.

For my first teaching job, I returned to Spanish Harlem, to the junior high I'd attended nine years before, where I'd been the only Anglo child in a class of Black and Latino children. I was a very, very bad teacher. I ran into the whole range of problems of how to bring order to a class. The adolescents knew exactly how to upset me, a green substitute. They were long used to incompetence in their teachers, and well able to take advantage of mine. They played on my white guilt and my desire to be considered a good person; only rarely did they respond to my earnest wish to show them new worlds. I began to get through to them during the Cuban missile crisis when I developed a lesson which evidently spoke to their need to be part of a larger world. It wasn't a sophisticated lesson, just some vocabulary work with the words that were in the air at the time, and map work comparing our country with the gnat that supposedly threatened it. But since I had no real insight about why the lesson worked, I didn't develop others like it.

So I felt really grateful to be rescued after six weeks by a call from principal Erwin Kaufman at Public School 123 nearby. He was looking for a substitute to cover a class of gifted fifth graders at his Harlem school. At that time "gifted" also meant orderly and docile, so although I was untrained and naive, still I managed to do a nice job of teaching interesting things, while avoiding the whole problem of how to keep children under what in public schools passes for control.

Kaufman kept me on next semester, this time to teach a regular class of fourth graders. Once more I experienced that shocking awareness, characteristic of new teachers, that I couldn't order the chaos, couldn't create an environment peaceful enough for learning (as I envisioned learning) to take place. I thought then that a teacher was supposed to teach things like reading and math. Today I think the teacher's job is also to create a workspace for children to live in and use to further their own education.

That term was terribly frustrating, and most afternoons I went home and wept. Many other teachers have since told me they did the same. We cried because all we had was vision: we had neither tools nor competence.

I got a fair amount of help from Mr. Kaufman, who observed that I kept getting lost in the details of organizing 35 children. He set me the task of creating routines so I could just keep school for a whole morning, not lifting a finger. He made me look at routines as a way of bringing order to the classroom.

So we set up what the children were to do first thing in the morning, what they were to do after that, and where they were to look for what to do after that. The children saw these new procedures as a struggle which I won if they obeyed, and they won if they disobeyed. But they were able to see that if we got together and cooperated, they won, too. It took about ten days until we settled for this last solution. The ensuing order and stability made room for me to start learning how to teach.

A wise resource teacher suggested that I encourage spoken language by having the children give a weekly panel show. She had me set up a "problem box" where children deposited notes they wrote about things that were bothering them. These problems could be signed or anonymous. Each Friday afternoon, a panel of five or six children would read and discuss what they found in the box. If the problem was signed its author could explain and get deeper into the discussion; if not, there was a lot of speculation as to whose it was, with some silliness and much gossip.

Foolishness aside, the children dealt with real issues like "I can't make my sister leave my stuff alone", or "My mother don't like my best friend." They gave each other a lot of kind and sometimes tender support and validation.

I inherited that fourth grade class midyear from a teacher who'd begun rehearsing the children in the musical comedy Peter Pan for the school assembly of some 1200 people. I was expected to direct, produce, costume, and play piano. At every rehearsal, everything went wrong. When the star couldn't find his green shorts and shirt "cuz somebody stole 'em" and announced, just before dress rehearsal, that he wouldn't accept any substitutes and was quitting the show, I finally sat down in the front row and cried.

Then our Captain Hook got up on stage and told the rest, "If anybody makes that teacher cry again, I'm gonna beat 'em up." Supported by this hero in villain's clothing, I managed to rise to the occasion, and we pulled it off, performing Peter Pan with a full musical score and the hero suitably attired in yet another costume!

My first experience with the overlap of real world politics and what goes on in the classroom had been during the Cuban missile crisis. The next incident opened my eyes to the damage racism can do to decent people who are trying to communicate.

One girl in that class went crazy every so often, and when I kept notes about these incidents I found that they occurred right after assembly or quite early in the morning, the times we said the Pledge of Allegiance. When I conferred with her parents they explained. "We're Black and we don't buy that garbage about 'one nation with liberty and justice for all'." They said they were open with their children about these opinions so their daughter must find it hard to deal with the hypocrisy of this ceremony. I excused the child from participating and saw her relax.

I taught in the New York City public schools for four years and in 1968-69, after our son Alexander Jeremy was born, took a Master's degree program in Early Childhood Education and Supervision at Teacher's College, Columbia.

Our "Experienced Teacher Fellowship Program" taught banal half-truths and generalities about children, curriculum, and survival, except for courses by Miriam Dorn and Sheila Sullivan, both of whom helped us to look for intelligent, humorous, respectful, realistic solutions to teaching problems.

In 1969 Ron Clemens and I adopted our second child, Jennifer Martine, and Ann Brown and I jointly founded The Discovery Room for Children, which I directed for two years, fighting City Hall while developing staff and program. (Other questions which came up then are discussed in Perspectives after Parts II and III.) The Discovery Room is still, in 1984, functioning. Many of my co-workers continue to teach there. Gwen Crenshaw, the present director, is the mother of Marcie, who was in our first class. Under her leadership staff members who had no degrees have gotten their BA's and increased their self-esteem, despite continuing bad treatment from the funding (and defunding) agency, New York's Department of Social Services.

Our family moved to San Francisco in 1971, and the next fall I began eight years of teaching four-year-olds in the prekindergarten at Burnett School in Bayview-Hunters Point.

II

Senses
and
Skills

What is it, then
To educate but
To develop these
Five
Divine germs
Called the senses?

—Thoreau

1

Knock, knock:
Getting the children's attention

"Can't you see?" shouted Piglet. "Haven't you got eyes? Look at me!"
—Winnie-the-Pooh

When I want to make a point, I sometimes use volume. If I raise or lower my voice, change pitch, sound magical or stern, the children focus on me. The situation reminds me of the man who sold a mule, promising that it would obey. The buyer got into the cart and said "Go," but the mule just stood there. He tried a few more times, then went back to complain. The seller went out to the mule, took up a handy two-by-four, and hit the mule, saying, "Go, go," and the mule started. The buyer protested, "But you said he'd obey!" The seller replied, "He does, he does, but first you have to get his attention!"

One of the best ways to have children come to attention quickly is to do something interesting the minute they are ready. (See the chapter on positive reinforcement for more on this.) Some of the children we encounter in group settings have learned, because it only brings trouble, not to come when called. We can turn this around by calling, insistently, firmly, even going and getting a child, and then presenting her with a treat.

While I don't use a two-by-four, I do like to avoid repeating myself endlessly, so I make sure I've captured the child's attention first. When I'm trying to communicate and feel resistance, what I do is say clearly, "Look at me. I'm talking to you." Once contact is established, I gladly speak in a normal voice. Being tough and real makes me a teacher the children believe in and learn from.

On the other hand, we mustn't bully children into stopping to listen to us when they're perfectly capable on their own. My friend Catherine Camp tells me that her son, Bayliss, when he was five years old, came home having made a crafts project. He had been to both Tot Town (his child care center) and his public school that day. Catherine asked Bayliss where the project had been done. He answered: "It's from school. She had to tell us how to do it. At school they always tell us how. At Tot Town we figure it out by ourselves."

2

Don't let the carpets smother your sound: Sensory preference

"Rabbit's clever," said Pooh thoughtfully.
"Yes," said Piglet, "Rabbit's clever."
"And he has Brain."
"Yes," said Piglet, "Rabbit has Brain."
There was a long silence.
"I suppose," said Pooh, "that that's why he never understands anything."

—The House at Pooh Corner

Children, like adults, are strikingly different in the senses they rely on most for communication. To see this in a personal way, try this exercise. Number a paper from one to five. List next to number one the sense through which you get the most *information* from your environment. Number two is the sense through which you get the next most information, and so forth. Please do this exercise before you read on.

Now number from one to five again, only this time rank your senses in the order in which you get *enjoyment* from your environment. Having done this, look and see what happened.

I've found that about ninety per cent of those who do this exercise list sight first in the information ranking. The other ten per cent list hearing first. There's a wider spread in the enjoyment ranking.

Since my auditory powers are dominant, my perceptions often differ from others'. Schools work best for folks like me. What do teachers do, if not talk? And expect you to remember what they said? This despite all the wisdom in our culture which tells us that a picture is worth a thousand words.

A case in point. There were two teachers working in a laboratory school. During the summer they had a wall removed between the two rooms so they could work jointly with a double class come fall.

They ordered some special supplies for September. These, of course, arrived late. Their teaching was amicable through the fall. They found they communicated well, enjoyed the same pace. In December their stuff arrived, including wall-to-wall carpeting, which made the room quieter.

By the end of January they were angry with each other. And by the end of February some friends had to help them reconcile their differences.

What was discovered, after considerable searching, was that one of the two was an auditory person. She had been depending on room noise to decide when to start moving her group of children in order to synchronize with her colleague. The carpets had largely silenced her source of information, leaving her feeling that the communication between her partner and herself had been subverted. The other teacher was primarily visual, so of course he had no idea what sort of trouble the carpet had caused. He felt that he had in no way changed, but she was now misreading him. As soon as they became aware of the sensory difference, they were easily able to bridge it, and once again they taught as a congenial team.

It's interesting to think about which sense you'd choose to lose in an accident, or which you'd choose to be deprived of from birth, or which ones you use when you dream or remember. A couple I know used to begin a discussion in bed, and then find it had turned into two arguments. The (visual) husband would argue that they must go into the living room and turn on the lights to pursue the argument sensibly. The wife (auditory) would hold out for staying warm in bed, with the lights off, because she couldn't see the point of lights and living room.

Because I am more auditory, I feel confident in assessing children's language. To validate my impression of their artwork, however, I seek other opinions. Several times a year I study one day's artwork in order to grow in my ability to judge the children's skill levels.

To teach children with precision, we must be aware of their strong senses and of our own. The only great strength we found in Terry was her graceful physical response to music. We used her love of movement to build her confidence in other areas. She learned to count in hopscotch patterns. She enjoyed reading more when the lessons involved crossing the circle of children to claim a word. She painted outdoors on big sheets of butcher paper.

Besides hearing, sight, touch, taste, and smell, we have a thermal sense, which estimates temperature without touching, and a kinesthetic sense, which lets us know the speed of a passing car. Both of these are used extensively by people handicapped in hearing or sight. The blind person turns the corner because he experiences both thermal and kinesthetic changes at the building line.

Some schools have heeded the sensory needs of children. Montessori and Froebel did, and so did the rabbis in the eastern European Cheders. When a child first entered the Jewish school he was given an alphabet spread with honey, to lick off, "so his first taste of learning should be sweet."

3

Movement:
Everybody's first language

*. . . Tigger was tearing around the Forest making loud yapping noises for Rabbit.
And at last a very Small and Sorry Rabbit heard him. And the Small and Sorry
Rabbit rushed through the mist at the noise, and it suddenly turned into Tigger; a
Friendly Tigger, a Grand Tigger, a Large and Helpful Tigger, a Tigger who
bounced, if he bounced at all, in just the beautiful way a Tigger ought to bounce.*

"Oh, Tigger, I am glad to see you," cried Rabbit.

—The House at Pooh Corner

English educators are wise to stress body movement for young children. In an
increasingly speeded-up world, they remind us that children need to be honored
for their physical development. We need to take the time to help each other do
things gracefully and naturally, not backwards or the hard way. If we help the
children be comfortable, graceful and balanced in their bodies they are also freer
to focus on concepts.

For a restful place in the day, we form a circle around a child sitting in a
chair, eyes bright, and perform a play-party song:

There sits Terry
In the chair chair chair
She's grown a whole lot
Since her birthday last year

So stand up on your feet
And find someone to greet
And (s)he'll be the next one
To sit upon the seat.

Simple exercises can have grand results. We tell the children to crouch down,
but still be on their feet. Then, slowly, we tell them they're balloons, and we're
going to blow them up, first their stomach, then their chest, then their arms, then
their hands, then their faces, then their ears, then their eyes, then their legs, then
their toes, then POP! and we all explode. At first it takes an adult to pace and
lead the game, later children do. At first there is a lot of wobbling and expand-
ing too fast, later children come to take pleasure in gradual unfolding.

The children often defeat themselves by immobilizing parts of their bodies so that what starts out difficult becomes impossible. Some brace one hand against the floor when sitting on the rug. This means their free hand gets no help from its partner, and they're always a little numb, off balance for many kinds of work. We rearrange children's bodies so they're more centered, with both hands free. We move them gently, saying, "Try sitting like this."

Children like to play kitties and doggies and snakes on the floor, and tall giraffes and roaring lions and big gorillas and whales eating little fish. Elephants, as we demonstrate to the children, are so big that it takes Lukash and Amanda to make one elephant. The two stand facing in the same direction, Amanda behind Lukash, and Amanda puts her arms around Lukash, clasping and extending them for a trunk. This is a good exercise for children who are afraid of touching. Situps are good for them too, with one child sitting on the feet of the other at first, and then an exchange of places.

Of course a thoughtfully equipped nursery classroom has a sturdy rocking chair for the teacher to cuddle children in, as well as little rocking chairs. This rocking motion isn't trivial; several religions incorporate rocking into praying. The rocking message needs to be clear: it's okay to need a little loving; we all do, sometimes. It's okay to take care of the baby inside; we all need that, too.

Here in San Francisco, where children can play outdoors about 165 of the 180 school days, we take the same care with the outdoor program that we do indoors. Usually Katherine takes the group out while I read with individuals in the classroom. Katherine keeps records of the children's achievements, encouraging them to improve their skills and learn new ones. The more agile children find techniques, and she uses these techniques to help the less adept. In autumn they work with tricycles, and when Lukash lifts up the trike to change its direction, Katherine helps him learn to steer. Others practice climbing, or negotiate over toys in the sand; later our low-slung, safe two-wheeler becomes the focus. They play with jump ropes, hula hoops, skates, and chalk; they blow bubbles, dance to recorded music, play rhythm instruments, and walk on stilts. This intensive outdoor program helps their bodies grow strong and makes it possible for children to be calm indoors when they have something hard to do.

Body movement is a first, tentative language. If we read children's messages from their expressive body English, we can often give them the English they need. We may know what a child wants from her shrug or look or movement toward an objective, but our policy is that people must ask for activities in words before they may do them. At the start of the year this means translating for many children. So when I see Leslie eyeing the blocks I tell her "Say, 'May I play with the blocks?'" and wait for her to repeat my words. With Millie I make it easier, "Say, 'I want blocks'." By spring she comes to me and announces, firmly, "Sydney, I want to play with the blocks. I have to make a store."

4

May I give you a hug?
Sex education

"That's my tablecloth," said Pooh, as he began to unwind Tigger.
"I wondered what it was," said Tigger.
"It goes on the table and you put things on it."
"Then why did it try to bite me when I wasn't looking?"
"I don't think it did," said Pooh.
"It tried," said Tigger, "but I was too quick for it."

—*The House at Pooh Corner*

We teach about sex mainly between Thanksgiving and Christmas, because sex is interesting and so that we don't have to listen to so much random talk about what Mama's going to buy them for Christmas.

We taught some of our classes about human reproduction, using a book called *How Babies Are Made*, (see Bibliography II) with pictures done in collage. I like the book because the babies are of all races, and the dogs and rooster and hen are shown explicitly copulating; but then the book chickens out and puts the human couple under a blanket. Last year, after what we felt was a nice solid unit on reproduction, one of the children asked Katherine to hand him up a book to the treehouse. "Which one?" she asked. "The nasty one!" he replied. So much for our countering social attitudes toward sex. Katherine made no comment, and that seems wise to me.

Even when we put out good information (see Bibliography I) and answer all questions, there's a feeling of being off the point with fours. Sexual intercourse is not the sexy subject for them. They're more concerned about what people in their families who copulate are doing to each other, about why they're kept out of it, about their bodies as sources of pleasure and pain, about what things girls are supposed to do and what things boys are supposed to do, about whether they are and will remain the way they were born, and about the shaming and strangeness of nudity.

We talk about our bodies, and learn a chant. I say, "What is Maurice?" The children answer, "Maurice is a boy." "What was Maurice when he was born?"

"He was a baby boy." "What will Maurice be when he grows up?" "He'll be a man." We go all around the circle of children and adults, and ask all these questions for each person. It isn't self-evident to the children that this generalization holds, and they find the exercise valuable.

In support of the general theme of being okay, we use the book, *What is a Girl? What is a Boy?* by Stephanie Waxman. Discarding all role, hair, and decoration aspects of boyness and girlness, it makes clear that a boy is a boy because he has a penis, and a girl is a girl because she has a vagina. This is the point to four-year-olds.

We want to be sure that the children learn several things that will help them struggle through the culture's confusions about sexuality. We want them to come to believe in their own perceptions. We want them to know that while there are things they may not do, there is nothing they are forbidden to feel. We want them to feel free to tell people not to touch them in uncomfortable ways. We want them to see that work can be separated from gender.

Two rules of thumb help me avoid teaching sexist stereotypes. 1) Substitute "Black" for "woman" and if one is racist the other's sexist. 2) Treat homosexuality the way you treat left-handedness, as a normal difference.

Some of our most beautiful children were being frightened by others "stealing" hugs and kisses. So one day when my son Alex was volunteering at school, during the circle I asked him to come over to me and I gave him a kiss. Then we all discussed why it was okay for me to kiss Alex without asking him, and made a list of people you can embrace without asking first. Then we went around the circle, each child asking another, "May I give you a hug?" or "May I give you a kiss?" Those asked were encouraged to answer either, "Yes, please" or "No, thank you."

Mister Rogers on PBS Television has lovely language for young children on this subject. He sings:

Everybody's fancy
Everybody's fine
Your body's fancy
And so is mine.

Our children get a lot of zest from this song. We all like being fancy.

5

Power over puzzles:
Toward successful problem-solving

"Lucky we know the Forest so well, or we might get lost," said Rabbit half an hour later, and he gave the careless laugh which you give when you know the forest so well that you can't get lost.

—*The House at Pooh Corner*

Puzzles can be used to help children feel better and better about their competence, but only if the children succeed, so the teacher needs to think clearly about increasing the likelihood of success. I recommend that puzzles be carefully chosen, be complete, be presented in order of difficulty, and be used with trays. None of these is necessary with one child at home, but all of them matter if a teacher wants to show children their progress through puzzling.

The first puzzle we give a child is a tree in four pieces that fit inside a frame. The trunk is all one piece, while the leafy top is cut into three distinctly-shaped pieces. I want to teach the child some routines for handling puzzles, and some skills for solving them. We look at the puzzle together and discuss the picture. Then I have the child dump the pieces onto a tray so we don't lose them or mix them up with another puzzle. Next I say, "Turn over the pieces so we can see the colors." For many children "turn over" has no meaning, so I repeat the words as I demonstrate with a first piece. When the child has turned the other pieces over, I say "Find one that will go in." They all choose the trunk, and put it in the right place. But after that some get stuck, with no idea how to go on. At this point I watch very closely to see how this child approaches a new problem. When I see that he or she is aware of being stuck, I offer help. If help is acceptable, I take over a little bit. The best time to intervene is when a child wants help.

Some kids look at a puzzle as if it can never get fixed.

The child with no attack skills needs to learn a lot of things. The most important is that you can control your puzzle. The most subtle may be that it's easier to find a piece to fit a place already identified than to pick up a piece at random and try to find a place for it.

As late in the year as November 27 we logged about Wesley:

Wesley does puzzles with neither hand leading, and with no apparent cooperation between his hands. He doesn't visualize how the piece will fit the space until he gets to the last piece.

A child thus thwarted is often gripping one piece in each hand and has stuck one or more where they don't belong in the puzzle. I have the child put all the pieces back on the tray. I take what I hope is the child's dominant hand. (It's early in the year and I'm often uncertain. I've heard that the thumbnail on one's dominant hand is wider than the other thumbnail, but I can't always see the difference. Parents occasionally tell me which hand is dominant, but sometimes they want to change a child's preference, so even that isn't always reliable.) The index finger of the hand I take is made to trace a distinctive part of the puzzle outline. Next, still holding the child's hand, I encourage the child to "look with your eyes and see if you can find the piece that will fit." Now I let the child work by trial and error.

One piece of the tree puzzle has only a small edge where it fits the outline. About six puzzles later, there are some with three or four interior pieces. If Leslie gets used to fitting the piece to the place, those later puzzles will not be so hard for her. After the first piece is fitted, I look for what Leslie perceives as necessary to finish the task. She is sufficiently informed and calmed by the first operation that she can sensibly put in a next piece, and a next. Others, before they realize that their random jabbings aren't working, need for weeks or months to be shown how to trace the puzzle edge and search for a complementary shape. Sometimes I find I must put the piece into the puzzle to prove to the child that it really can be controlled and made to fit, but when I do I always remove it and hand it to the child to replace.

Over the years at Burnett I sorted the puzzles from easiest to hardest, four to 28 pieces. This small-step sequence allowed most of the children to solve all 55 of the school's puzzles by spring vacation. After that, the children are free to take out any puzzle and do it again, and I sometimes put out a 50-piece UNICEF puzzle for us to work on collectively.

We need to be careful and patient when looking with a child at any problem, breaking it down into its constituent parts, and giving the child useful help. How confusing it must be to hear the two locutions I use in teaching puzzles: "Turn it around" and "Turn it over". Even though the distinction is fine, the children learn it, because I always show them what I mean as I say it.

When Leslie finishes her puzzle, I say, "Great! Now, do you want to do it again?" Probably she'll say yes; and when she's completed it a second time we say, "Was it easier this time? Do you want to do it again?" One day in September Lukash did three puzzles six times each before he'd had enough. When he finished each one we asked if he wanted it again, if he wanted a harder puzzle, or if he wanted something else. When he finished all those hard puzzles, Lukash was proud of himself.

6

Math:
Ways to think about problems

. . . and the big one came out first, which was what he had said it would do, and the little one came out last, which was what he had said it would do, so he had won twice . . . and when he went home for tea, he had won thirty-six and lost twenty-eight, which meant that he was—that he had—well, you take twenty-eight from thirty-six, and <u>that's</u> what he was. Instead of the other way round.

—The House at Pooh Corner

They used to say you needed math to balance your checkbook or to check on the supermarket clerk. I'm convinced that with automatic cash registers and money dispensing machines most people these days have little practical need to know such mathematics. Some people experience math as a roadblock subject they need to get through in order to finish school. Others find it an intrinsically rewarding thing to do with their minds as they discover the different kinds of order in the universe.

Most of us first learned math from elementary school teachers who were, themselves, uncomfortable with it. If we don't manage to come to terms with math, we will perpetuate this problem, but if we find calm and knowledge we can break the cycle, giving children tools that were hard for us to come by. Mathematicians often talk about their work as elegant. We have an obligation to start children off in such a way as to enable them to encounter this elegance.

I was never very good at math until as an adult I took some good courses on how to teach it. I think the key for me is that I mustn't teach children ways to *answer* problems, but rather ways to *think about* them.

So, instead of working with numerals, either spoken or written, we begin by making many picture charts that show quantitative relations. After reading a story with a big family in it, we chart our family sizes, putting stick figure families across the bottom of a chart, and listing the name of each child whose family size matches in the column above the picture.

As we finish giving foot rubs we make a chart that shows that Amanda and Leslie were wearing tights, Deena and Dinah were wearing long socks, and all

57

the other children were wearing short socks. We may discuss whether to add two more columns, one for Katherine, who is wearing stockings, and one for me, barefoot in my cloth shoes. (See the Nuffield Math book listed in Bibliography I for further ideas on pictographs.)

We teach children to count in settings where knowing how many serves a purpose. So, before we start out on a field trip, the children count off. We help those who need it, but since we have most of our field trips in the spring, it usually works pretty well. Children who need help with learning to count are referred to Sesame Street, and we all learn to say "One, two, buckle my shoe" as part of our language/music/math program. We may examine an orange to see how many seeds are in each segment, and we count jumprope jumps, because when Wesley has completed twenty he must give the rope to Deena who is waiting for a turn. We use a timer to help with turns, too, and some of the objective quality of five-minute turns may communicate itself to children as an interesting facet of measurement.

Concepts are built into the materials children play with. There are graduated cylinders, nesting cups, and the wonderful Cuisenaire and Dienes materials, each giving us a number system we can hold and manipulate.

I have a lot of respect for Montessori's number apparatus. She used gold-colored beads, on wires of one to ten beads each, with tens wired together to make hundreds, and hundreds wired together to make thousands. In Montessori's tenement nurseries, the two- to five-year-olds handed each other three hundred or one thousand beads, naming them. Presumably these children understood a number like one thousand two hundred four more deeply than do children who haven't handled a tangible hundred.

Montessori's geography materials started with a map of the world, went on to continent maps, and worked down to maps of Rome, the home of her program. Her books taught me to analyze learning so that more and more I start with what's large and go on to small. The first reading my children do is of very large writing, the first dominoes they get are on large blocks, and generally the objects on the shelves in the fall are larger than those in the spring.

The best block building by fours I've ever seen came when I presented only the largest, hollow blocks in the fall, added a set of large cardboard blocks after winter vacation, and only late in the year gave the children the unit blocks that are standard in nursery classrooms. The first buildings, generally the work of one child, were solid, straight walls. Later two and three children learned to build together. When I put a wheel in the area, a surge of vehicle building began. When green paper money appeared, stores were built. In January, with the addition of the cardboard boxes, the buildings became very tall. When the children were given the unit blocks, they used them purposefully from the first day.

All the best thinking in early childhood education tells us that little children learn what they experience through their senses; that they can't learn in abstract form. If you want to teach them about fire, you take them over to the stove. This is very important in math, where rote learning can be destructive for years to come. So when children count, they must count *things*. I find that with fours it's almost always better to have them move the things they are counting, so that they see that we assign a numeral to each item we count. There are some children whose poor coordination impedes their ability to move pieces while they count. We have them count as we put things into their hands. It's better to do this with a little push, so they feel the item as they count it.

Some children can count numbers. When you ask "Tell me, how many blocks do you have?" they start, "One, two, three, four, five." But if you then ask "How many?" they're stumped. They know the poem of number names, but it's a nonsense rhyme to them. They know you're supposed to count when asked how many, but they don't know that the last number has special significance, as the sum or size of the group of objects.

We play a counting game with plastic teddy bears. You can keep as many bears on your tray as you can count accurately. You ask the child on your right for, say, four bears. You put them with your old bears and count them all. If you count them correctly you may keep them until the child on your left asks you for some. The cautious children learn to ask for just one more, thus improving their chances of keeping what they've collected. Rash children, who covet more bears than they can count, are quickly chastened.

With first graders I have used and enjoyed Lore Rasmussen's *Miquon Math Materials*, which enable children to work at their own paces with Cuisenaire rods and other age-appropriate materials. Out of print for a long while, they are now available from Key Curriculum Project, P.O. Box 2304, Berkeley, CA 94702. A catalog is available.

While seeking a way to teach sameness and difference to fours, I stumbled onto a pleasing piece of logical language. It goes, "They're both markers, but they're not the same color. This one is red, and this one is blue." Or "They're both sticks, but they're not the same size. This one is short and this one is long." We also use heavy and light, hardback and paperback, curved and straight in this exercise. Some children, when presented with a new pair of materials, can change from "color" to "size" without being prompted.

This kind of exercise links math and language, and it even prepares the children for standardized testing. What's delightful is how much the children enjoy this kind of reciting. Amanda takes great pride in distinguishing light blue from dark blue in the exercise, and Millie is proud too when she says a simpler form right.

If a child gives a wrong answer, but seems sure it's right, try to puzzle out what question she's answering. Then ask that question, and you'll likely get the right answer to the first question in reply. So, with an older child, when you ask "Please tell me what two plus three is" and Gena tells you six, your next question is "Okay, so what do you think two times three is?" and she will answer "Oh, Oh, five!" With fours it might be "What comes after six?" "Eleven." "So what comes after ten?"

Similarly, if Lukash is stumped by a question like "Will you tell me what color this is?" you can make it more approachable by asking, "Is it red or yellow?" You can give him contrasting options (red or yellow) or close ones (gold or yellow) and use what you know about Lukash's knowledge to reduce his chances of failure. That is, if he has learned red, then asking him "Is this red or blue?" enables him to answer correctly.

I feel good when I'm able to help children enjoy solving mathematical problems—here's a subject I always had trouble with at school, and I'm pleased when the children aren't led to repeat my failure.

7

Spontaneous and unrehearsed: Listening and speaking

. . . you can't help respecting anybody who can spell TUESDAY, even if he doesn't spell it right; but spelling isn't everything. There are days when spelling Tuesday simply doesn't count.

—*The House at Pooh Corner*

I value language more than any other tool. One of the imbalances in power among people is their differing ability to use language. For four-year-olds, struggling for power over their lives, being able to name things and feelings and call them into being out of nowhere seems to be as powerful as, say, piloting an airplane. How can one relate feelings to ideas except through language? What else can you do with feelings that can't be acted out, but sit on them or stew in them and suppress them?

Because language begins with listening, we tape record stories for children, so they can listen to fine stories as many times as they want, without exploiting the adults or hearing the boredom that creeps in when we've read the same one too often. (See Bibliography II.) If I know it will spare me hundreds of repetitions, I'm capable of giving one great performance of a story for a tape, the best piece of theater I can produce, quick-paced and interesting even for children raised on television cartoons.

Whenever I see one of our fourteen dog-eared copies of *Curious George Rides a Bike* I'm glad I have a tape of the story. It's developmentally perfect for the children, who choose it and choose it, but it sure is developmentally wrong for me, and I used to *hate* reading it to the children. Of course, we do read stories to the children almost every day, and discuss and act them out often. The tapes are there to extend that experience.

The stories we choose to tape should be very interesting to the children. They should model some complexity and a wide range of language use, and their vocabularies should challenge the children. You can interrupt to define a hard word, or have the children repeat it, but generally the context will inform them, and they will pick up language just as they have right along.

When making a tape, work in a quiet environment. Establish a starting place for the children either by pasting a star on the first page, or by describing a picture there. When you're taping for young children you can ask them questions, and they'll answer the machine. This is helpful if you're across the room and want clues that they're involved. So you start by saying: "The name of this book is *Corduroy*. Say that with me: 'Corduroy.' Did you say 'Corduroy'? If you said 'Corduroy,' you said it right! Look for the page with the red circle with green overalls in it." (Pause.) "Did you find the overalls? Turn the page. Here is the story. 'Corduroy is a bear who once lived in the toy department of a big store . . . .' " Read to the end of the first page and say, "Turn the page."

We show children who are new to books how to turn pages from front to back. Some need to practice this skill with an adult, away from the tape recorder, until it is familiar. Five or six lessons of three minutes each will teach the slowest four-year-old the principles of page turning. Their interest in the illustrations helps.

Visiting parents are often interested in listening to tapes with their children. Since we want them to read to the children at home we show them how to pace, how to question, and especially how to let the magic of the story flow without interruption. When they see their children engrossed in stories, they find the prospect of reading aloud more attractive.

Because children listening to the tape recorder don't need much adult supervision, you can use the stories to separate children from the group and make it smaller. When you have a lesson that is inappropriate to a few children, you can send those few to the tape recorder while you teach the others.

Some children who love tapes listen every day, while others never choose it. If hearing stories is a priority, as with us, it's good to keep a checklist of story names and children's names next to the machine. We want each child to have heard each of our thirty taped stories at least twice during the year.

In addition to hearing stories, children can learn long or complicated songs from the tape. When Daphne was absent for two weeks just before graduation, we sent a tape on vacation with her, so she'd be up to date when she got back.

When Maurice was in the hospital, we all recorded messages to him, and Katherine and I took the tape and recorder with us to visit. This was a special, warm gift for Maurice. He asked to hear the tape twice more before we left.

We put our children's voices on tape in the fall, and listen for their comfort with language. Again in the spring, we tape their voices. They use the tapes to enjoy their voice images, and we use the tapes to analyze what we need to teach. Some subjects that seem always to evoke language are pets and other animals, clothing, what you like to do at school, family, and places you like to go. Parenthetically, I think this is one excellent way to assess the work of a teacher of young children. The teacher should make a tape in the fall, talking with each child for, say, ten minutes, and again in the spring. If the children don't show longer sentence patterns, more verbal assertiveness, more information, and some ability to use the teacher as a resource person, then she or he should be retrained or dismissed. If they do well, let the teacher be rewarded in salary, status, or both.

Speaking skills go along with the listening skills the children are developing. The most valuable classroom technique for developing speech is to listen carefully to what a child is saying, and to act on it. This is why we ask children again and again to tell us what they want to do. The child who gets results by talking is very apt to speak up.

We also try to describe what we see. From the log:

December 8. Ron tried a new game, called "What Happened?" He asks the children to describe the objects on a "stage" made from a box with a curtained front and open back. The curtain goes down, he rearranges objects and then says, "Open the curtain and tell me What Happened." Some children describe faithfully what's there now without reference to the prior situation. Some grasp the discontinuity and actually report what changed: "the doll got laid down" or "the ball's moved over." They even manage "There was three blocks before, and now there's only two."

Lucretia runs up to me and says "Monika said a bad word!" I squat down and ask, "What word did she say?" I think you have to examine your own deepest feelings about angry language before you can effectively teach children ways of dealing with it. I suspect Lucretia is excited by the word, so I give her a chance to say it if she likes, in a safe setting.

If that's not enough, I ask her how she felt when Monika said that. We name the feeling together, and I suggest that she tell Monika how she feels. Some phrasings that occur are: "I don't like it when you say those words." Or, "Don't you call me a ------, it makes me mad!" If Lucretia needs me at her side to have the courage to tell this to Monika, I go with her.

For me, words like "nigger," "spic," and "kike" aren't in the same category as other insults. I see them as weapons and treat them that way, telling children, "That word is only used for hurting people. This is a safe school, and I can't let you use words that make people feel so hurt." I isolate a child who won't stop using these words, but children don't persist in the face of my righteous anger. They are usually willing to respect what I hold precious, in exchange for my keeping them safe.

Many of our children are fluent in some modes of speech but stuck, sometimes quite badly, in others. Lukash can't bear waiting to use a new toy. He and Lamar got into a terrible fight over a brand new water wheel, and Katherine told them they couldn't have the wheel any more that day. Lukash went far away and did other things to avoid the misery of his deprivation. Lamar, on the other hand, sat and watched the other children play with it. When Amanda offered it to him he told her, "I'm not supposed to, cause I wasn't sharing it, and Katherine says I can't play with it today." Although Lamar can tell such a complicated story when generating his own language, he gets stuck when asked a question, and answers in monosyllables. It's hard for him to carry a message.

I tell Millie, "Tell Katherine I'm ready to start the meeting." Late in the year this is easy for Millie, but still hard for Lamar.

Deena tells me, "I want to play with flashlights." This is easy for Deena and Lamar, but hard for Millie.

Buck is in the dollhouse talking at length on the toy telephone. He says, "Hi man whatcha doin'? How's it goin' witchoo? I'm a-gonna call the po-leece and dey's gonna getchoo." This call isn't intended as communication with anyone in the room. Buck is expressing stuff he carries, and swaggering a bit. This is easy for Buck or Lamar, but hard for Millie or Deena.

I often give children language to repeat when they've tried to get me to do all the talking, while they just point or say "yeah" or "uh-huh". After I've determined what Kathye wants, I tell her "Say, 'Sydney, I want to climb on the dome.' " Millie, who has taken too much food, dawdles and picks. I ask, "Do you have too much food?" She nods. "Then tell me, 'I took too much.' " As soon as she repeats I say, "Go throw it away. Just take a little next time." Lukash is pulling on one end of a bike, Buck on the other. I interview both and tell them what to say. Lukash must tell Buck he wants a turn, and Buck must tell Lukash he'll come give him the bike when he's done with it. Most children repeat my words quite faithfully, especially when they see that saying the words gets quick action, not only from me but from other kids as well.

To help them discover the music in their own speech, I took out the drum at a meeting. Daphne said, "Somebody's outside crying." I drummed bum biddy bum bum BUM bum, twice, then added my voice, "Somebody's outside crying." The children joined in the chant. After about a dozen times, I broke the rhythm, now drumming and chanting, "Oh, dear, it's sad to be crying!" and we chanted that for a while. Then I asked the children to listen silently to the drum, and beat the first rhythm again. When I asked, "What's that?" Hamid told me immediately, "Somebody's outside crying."

Other fine language experiences for children come from hearing stories and joining in on their choruses, and from discussing stories and acting them out. I won't write about that here, since there's already much excellent material on these topics on any nursery school reference shelf. (See Huber, Tway, Arbuthnot, and Hearne in Bibliography I.) It's a pleasure to tell the story about *Sam* (see Scott, in Bibliography II) and, at the end, hear Lukash explain that Sam cried "cause he didn't have nobody to play wit."

In the Montessori exercise where the children "make a Silence" we all listen to the sounds that come through the silence. During a Silence of two minutes we heard a child in the playground threatening to tell on another, and we heard a motorcycle and a truck and a cough, and somebody in the circle wiggled, so we heard that, too. I occasionally tape the sounds made during a Silence, so we can replay them to build further acuity.

Sometimes the children's hearing is a pleasure, and sometimes it is so selective it drives me nuts. I was working on a movement exercise with the children in a circle. I wanted them to sit down where they were standing, so we could go on without re-forming the circle. I said, "Please sit down right where you are." They all went back to their original places on the rug. Since this is a direction I give often and want understood, I took a deep breath and decided to teach it. Patiently, I had them get back into the circle. I asked reliable children, one by one, to "sit down right where you are." Two children, despite having seen five or six others do what was expected and be complimented for it, persevered through several repetitions of mis-hearing. What do they get from this sort of disconnection from other people?

After we had accomplished the seated circle, Deena said to me "Let's get in our circle." I was confused, but then I thought I saw what she meant. So I asked them to reach out to the children on either side and take hands again. Deena smiled, relaxing because now we really had a circle.

8

Mama, monster, muscle, money: Reading what means most

"It's a Missage," he said to himself, "that's what it is. And that letter is a 'P,' and so is that, and so is that, and 'P' means 'Pooh,' so it's a very important Missage to me, and I can't read it. I must find Christopher Robin or Owl or Piglet, one of those Clever Readers who can read things, and they will tell me what this missage means . . . ."

—*Winnie-the-Pooh*

Children feel that learning to read is a special, grownup thing to do. And they know that they're supposed to learn to read at school. Young children have intimate experience with words—at four, they're mastering the immense task of learning a human language. It's vital to start from this strength. They have strong feelings: love, hate, fear. Our reading program helps them get in touch with these feelings and deal comfortably with them.

Reading experts seem to feel that you must use many methods to teach children to read. I have no argument with this. My son learned to read at three by Sylvia Ashton-Warner's method as explained below and my daughter really caught on to reading when she was given phonics at school. However, no matter how many systems you employ, you must still fit the system to each child.

Parents are often anxious to have their children achieve academically. From this anxiety can come pressures that may actually defeat such achievement. Parents need to be able to perceive their children as smart, productive, and "good at school."

Teaching children to read helps them gain the respect of their parents. Parents are virtually unanimous in their delight when they hear that I plan to teach their four-year-olds to read. They are moved to smiles and tears of joy when they first hear their children reading words, and are particularly pleased with the children's confidence.

When I teach reading, parents allow me a lot of latitude for a play curriculum because it seems to them that I must know what I'm doing. (An excellent book on the importance of play is *The Complete Book of Children's Play* by Ruth

Hartley. See Bibliography I.) Reading is the only child's skill that universally impresses adults in our culture. It's what children go to school to learn.

Since we're not required to teach four-year-olds to read, it's our responsibility at least not to turn them off by our reading lessons.

These ideas stand behind what Ashton-Warner calls the Key Reading Scheme as I've come to use it.

In each of the classes I've taught in San Francisco, all the four-year-olds learned to read fifteen to ninety words. And all felt happy about learning to read. Some had to struggle mightily for the first six weeks or so to catch on. Others suffered setbacks because their parents brought them to school only intermittently. But they all learned to read in a clear, confident way.

This way of teaching reading requires the teacher to know the children well enough to evoke from them the words that trigger their emotions. Reading their own words helps the children experience increasing interest, pleasure, and power. A word that truly captions an emotion is read spontaneously the way the child learned to speak it two or three years earlier. A child whose primary relationship is with Mama will learn to read "mama" early.

Starting Them Off

How do you get children started reading? You begin the first lesson by saying "Maurice, I think you're ready to learn to read! Watch this." And you print "Maurice" very big on an envelope which will hold all his words. Now ask, "Tell me what that says."

If he answers correctly, say "That's one word you can already read!"

Help him find his next word by talking with him a little before you ask "Tell me about the people in your house. Who takes care of you?" Only after his tongue is a bit loose do I ask the clincher, "Tell me whom you love best in the whole world." You may have to coach him: "Who gives you big hugs? Who makes you good things to eat?" Each year one or two children, seeking the right answer, say they love me best. This is before we know each other very well, and I see it as a mistaken expectation of what the teacher wants. One of our teaching goals is to strengthen children so they stop giving answers that undercut their own truth.

When Maurice chooses a word that rings true, print it on a card. Give the word to him, telling him to hold it in both hands and look at it. Then take back the word, put it on the table with the envelope, and ask Maurice, "Give me the one that says 'Maurice' . . . Good, that's 'Maurice'. Now give me 'mama' . . . Good, you know both words. If you know them both next time I'll give you a new one."

Pitfalls of the first lesson: 1) You print the name on the envelope and the child fails to identify it. Offer a choice: "Is it Maurice or Tommy?" 2) You tell him to give you "mama" and he gives you "Maurice". Say "Slow down. Keep your hands in your lap and just look at the words." Try to figure out why he's wrong if he perseveres in his error. If he's so eager that he can't stop to think, slow him down. If he's distracted, end the lesson pleasantly. "We'll read tomorrow when you're ready to work hard for a little while." Consider the possibility that he may be answering a different question than the one you're asking. Try: "That word says 'mama' but I said to give me 'Maurice'. Give me 'Maurice'."

The first dozen lessons shouldn't take longer than four minutes each, and by year's end they should still be no longer than 12 minutes.

Early lessons are private time between teacher and one child. At first the words will be selected by your perceptions and guiding questions:

Who do you love best?

What's the scariest thing you can think of?

What do you like to eat?

What do you like to have in your pocket?

Start the second lesson by saying, "I bet you remember both your words. Tell me your words." Help if he falters or forgets. "Now, I want you to touch 'mama.' Good! Now touch 'Maurice.' Wow! You really can read your words. Close your eyes and we'll find another good word for you to read. Can you tell me what's really scary?" After the new word is chosen, play two games with all the words. First you name a word and Maurice touches it, then you ask "What's this?" and he names the word you touch.

The Words Come From Inside

Your task is to help the child pick words that are deeply felt, and to dismiss irrelevant words with protests or giggles. I ask children to close their eyes while we search, so they don't just name the first thing they see. Some children, like Ivan, are in close touch with their emotions, but most are too inhibited to say "I want a word that says 'peepee,' " or "I want 'whipping'."

Where do the words come from? From inside the children.

By winter break the most mature children are finding words without my probing and prompting, and by the end of the year few need much help. As they get to know their own minds, they become able to articulate their experience and demand just what they need. No matter where Amanda has learned to read a word, when I discover she can read it, it goes with the others in her envelope. But my insight also brings words to them that can heal or empower. Noticing Lucretia's anxiety about being small for her age, I suggest words like "strong" or "muscle" to her. Suggesting this kind of deficit-filling word continues to be my job throughout the year.

Alert children spot words around the classroom. The green paper money has "money" written on it. The doctor stuff is in a kit marked "doctor." Names of the children are written on everything they draw, paint, write or dictate. These are displayed as the room's main decorations.

Activity choices help me know which words to suggest. Those who choose to play in the darkened bathroom with flashlights usually want "dark," "dry," "light," "night," and "moon." Those who play TV at length in the dollhouse and in the yard want "Superman," "Batman," "Wonder Woman," "Incredible Hulk," and "Mickey Mouse." Those who are chubby and chatty want "french fries," "coconut cake," "mustard," "candy," "ice cream," and "hot sauce." Those who always know what's going on in the class read all the other children's names by January. Such social children may read 40 proper nouns in a deck of 60 words by the end of the year.

Kids who can read all the other children's names get special jobs: they put away paintings and notices in the children's cubbies, matching names on paintings with names on the cubbies. This kind of distribution takes place a lot, and children selected to do it feel proud.

I don't censor the choice of words except by being as sure as possible that the word has emotional weight for the child. It can be any word at all. Remember, it takes time to locate a real Key Word: one that labels emotion, unlocks feelings. You'll find out a lot about each child's self-knowledge by observing whether he or she chooses words that "stick" or ones that are soon forgotten. Make an agreement with each child to throw away any words that don't stick, or you'll be setting up both the child and yourself for failure.

Amanda read her uncle Harry's name for months, but then she had a fight with him and forgot how to read "Harry." We threw it away. That's a very important part of this kind of reading. Any word Amanda keeps forgetting she throws in the wastebasket, as I remind her: "We just want to keep the words you really know how to read." What constitutes forgetting varies according to the person, but if a word doesn't stick by the fourth time that's too much.

About the second time a child forgets a word, I say, "If you don't know it next time, let's throw it away." For some children that warning is enough to insure that they'll know it next time. Another way we encourage focus is to ask, "Do you want to learn it, or do you want to throw it away?" Children see things they aren't good at as traps. There are no traps in our reading lessons.

Scheduling and Recording Lessons

Try to give each child at least two lessons a week. At four minutes a lesson, for 20 children, this comes to less than three hours of your time per week. If you have each child send you the next one, you can use the time between children to record your lesson on a simple chart like this:

Date	Style/manner/problems	New word	Word Dropped	Count
12/6	Confident, forgot jelly.	Godzilla		7
12/9	Sleepy, forgot jelly.		jelly	6
12/12	Together, 100%.	tiger		7
12/16	Confuses tiger/bigger.			7
12/18	Clear, 100%.	earthquake		8

When children ask me for additional lessons, I try to honor their requests. Occasionally a child needs a lesson every day, to move ahead. As the year goes on, I sometimes have children hear each other's words if I'm busy. These lessons often are perfectly serious and helpful to both teaching and learning child.

The Second Stage—Sentences

The third game in our reading sequence is when I ask Maurice, referring to his words on the table, "What are you going to give me?" and he must respond, "I'm going to give you 'mama'." This time he's choosing which word to deal with and speaking a sentence, in addition to reading. The fourth game is the hardest and is the children's favorite: in it I am passive, and the child plays teacher, telling me "I want you to give me 'hot sauce'," and telling me if I'm right or wrong (I make many mistakes!) and generally being in charge. Here Maurice is identifying his words, making decisions, articulating commands—and to a grownup! I refuse to understand when he speaks too fast or runs words together past normal recognition. When he says "I wannoogimmee," I make him separate the words. He needn't always speak slowly, but he needs to know what to do when someone says "I can't understand you." We teach him that it sometimes helps to articulate, especially with people who don't know him well. He also benefits as a reader if he comes to know separate words, and not just phrases. Deena can have "Incredible Hulk" only if she works to pronounce it correctly, instead of saying "crebeluk" with her eyes as wide as saucers, the way she did when she asked for it.

When Lukash has about 12 words, I add a verb to connect them. Since all his words are people's names, I offer "loves" or "likes" so we can make three word sentences: "Lukash loves mama," or "mama loves Lukash." We don't begin sentences with capital letters at this stage of reading, since that would involve changing the look of the word, and we want those looks to remain dependable. And since most printed matter is in lower case, we use upper case only to begin proper names.

If the words name toys, I suggest "plays": "Leslie plays house," or "Leslie plays bike." Hamid's taste runs to monsters, so I give him "scary" to make "scary Godzilla," "scary Frankenstein."

Here are some sentences from the end of the year:

Allen loves to look at cartoons. Suzanne loves to play doll house. I like to dress up fancy. Allen loves to swing. Victor can play Frankenstein. (Allen is obedient and articulate.)

Cherry loves mama. Cherry hit Manny. stop it, Cherry. stomach sick. stomach well. (Cherry is angry, repressed, has an autistic older brother.)

Paul dry. hot, hot night. Batman hot. robber hot. robber eating. Santa Claus eating. (Large, gentle boy. Four, and oldest of four children.)

Amanda is painting a beautiful picture. yes, mama eats chicken and spaghetti. people can skip and laugh and go. a big beautiful blue and purple monster. (Amanda's very good at school. She likes the kinds of things that happen here.)

I am fast Harry, little and sharp. I like to play football and basketball. Harry loves mama and daddy. (Harry is just like he says.)

Tinka sees a dome and an airplane. Keith is always a baby. my mama Yuriko hugs and loves me. you are my fancy family. (Tinka's Korean-Black, living with her mama, daddy, and Keith, the baby. She's more active than many children, and very, very acute in her perceptions.)

The children don't make up the sentences. Since they don't know exactly what sentences are, they can't be told to construct them. When Jason is ready to read sentences, I set up his cards so they generate thinkable combinations, and tell him "read all these words." If he likes a sentence, it goes into a book for further reading. Thus, though Jason doesn't create his sentences, he does approve them.

This reading system works better than either traditional system in common use: better than phonetic analysis, and better than the Dick-and-Jane type of controlled vocabulary programs. Phonetic analysis has two major drawbacks: English spelling is not regular, and children of this age are not dependably analytical. The trouble with the Dick-and-Jane kind of reader is that it's dull, dull, dull. So there's no reason to bother to figure it out. The Ashton-Warner method uses a controlled vocabulary of the most exciting words, and requires only recognition, not analysis. The sentences I compose from the children's words are about the most vivid community, people, activities, monsters, fears, and fantasies these children can voice.

Writing

The children have stories to tell, they dictate them to us, and when they're written down they are hung on the walls. The stories almost always include some reading words, born of the children's lives.

Leslie's Story about Earthquakes

The dome is a magic dome, cause it's got a earthquake in it. And it has magic fireman hats. When you put the fireman hats on it makes the earthquakes go away.

And then all the boys was happy. And then the girls came out and said, "Where's my earthquake?"

And then the mama came out and said, "Where's my earthquake, my honey earthquake."

Buck's Story about the Zoo

I went to see some animals. I went with the people from my school. Ivan, Jeffrey, Sydney and me looked at the animals, and I loved the horsie. I saw a baby pig and a mama. I didn't know they was pigs. My teacher told me.

I saw a baby spider monkey in a mama's lap. Spider monkeys was tiny. I saw some gorillas and I saw their little red teeth.

I pushed by myself on the swing. A big boy scared me on the train. I had a good zoo trip.

Cat Story by Lawrence

I like this cat and this cat and this cat. They say miaow. They're soft. They're on a rug. A cat would play with me. Play football, basketball: "Lawrence, now you kick it." I play basketball on a shoe court outside.

We also build charts of our mutual experiences. Here's one we made after observing daffodils for several weeks:

Daffodils

Terry said "The big flower smells like potatoes."
Amanda said "The big flower smells good."
Wesley said "The big flower smells like bubble gum."
Lukash said "The big flower's pretty."
Ivan said "The big flower smells delicious."
Jeffrey said "The yellow flower is big."
Daphne said "The white flower is little."
Leslie said "The white flower has three flowers."
Dinah said "The big flower has one flower."
Millie said "The big flower nice."
Hamid said "The big flower got three leaves."
Deena said "The big flower got green leaves."
Maurice said "It smell like sugar gum."
Marie said "The flowers are very good."
Buck said "The flower smell like sugar."

Tinka said "The flower look like sugar."
Kathye said "The flower just like sugar."

We look for ways that children can share their reading vocabularies. Sometimes a word is in fashion. From the log:

October 20. Block building is more and more excellent—a "super" series was built: "supertrain," "superplane," and even "superbatmobile!" I offered to give the kids the word "super" and six or seven came and got it. Buck valued his "super" word so highly that he still was holding on to it after an hour in the park.

After New Year's other children tend to hang out at the reading table, admiring each other's reading and picking up words of interest.

I sometimes make a book that collects everybody's food words, or scary words, or family words. During the period when we're making sure all the children learn all the names, I make a book with photos of the children. The most cheerful of these was a belly-button book, with a photograph on each page of a child showing his or her navel. My friend Marcie Wollesen gave me this lovely idea. This book is read round-robin at meetings.

I've also taken to writing the children's names on the backs of their word cards, so I can pick out a few words from each envelope, shuffle them together, and lay them all out on the floor. Children raise their hands when they see a word they know, come up and read it aloud, and return with it to their places. When Terry reads a word with Amanda's name on the back she gives it to Amanda. When all the words are claimed the game is over.

The children are proud to show their reading to each other and to their parents. Every five words or so we send home some words stapled together to make a book, for the children to read to their families. To help parents use the material that comes home, we attach a dittoed letter asking them to keep reading sessions short, and to simply tell the children words they forget. The note reminds them that if they don't review reading with the children over the holidays, the children may lose ground.

The first books we make have one word on each page; later ones may have as many as three short sentences:

Lukash loves mama
I ride two-wheeler
run scary monster

All the writing—word cards, names on work, sentences, books—is done in letters that are neat, consistent, and BIG! There's some question about abusing the eyes of children this young, and writing with tall letters about two inches high and short ones about one inch seems to remove any physical strain from the task. If children have been taught to write and read their names in upper case only, we tell them that that's their name, and there's another way to write their name, too. As the year progresses and many children can print their names, I take a big piece of chartboard and write at the top, "I can write my name," and then paste on the children's lovely scrawly signatures. I learned to paste on the names after kids scribbled out errors on nearly done charts. We have to get around children's perfectionism any way we can!

When a child can write both first and last names, we make a special trip to the library to apply for a library card.

Teaching Writing

I teach writing along with reading because children learn to read faster when they are also learning to write the same words, because some children are very eager to write, and because parents place a high value on writing. On the other hand, you may choose not to teach writing because it's time-consuming, it's difficult for some children, or you don't feel eager to teach it.

Here's how I teach writing. First determine the child's dominant hand. Before children can form their own letters, let them trace yours. Begin with the child's first name, writing it big with a fine line marker or pen or pencil. Since many children grip a writing tool like a dagger or a paintbrush, show them how to hold the fat marker like a pencil and to put the other hand on the edge of the paper to keep it from slipping. Put the writing hand so the marker point is at the top of the first letter, then observe the child's way of beginning. Don't intervene too quickly. Note inefficiency or awkwardness to discuss later, but only after you're sure you know what you want to say. Most children can trace the same model many times, and some like to do that in many colors. I'm firm that they must work from left to right in sequence, and that they mustn't change hands mid-word and spoil the rhythm. Otherwise I let them experiment pretty freely.

When I feel a child is ready to write systematically, I offer suggestions:

"It's easier if you start that letter at the top."

"Little *E* is a hard letter to write. Here are some to practice on. You start with this straight line in here, then finish up with the round part."

For the lower case *A*, "First make the round part, starting here," indicating the top, "then make the stick."

"First make the round part, then the tail," for lower case *G*.

"It all looks clear but the *Y*. Here's a bunch of *Y*s for you to write on. Make the little part first, then the big part."

By mid-year our children have mixed reading-writing lessons. First they pick up the words from the table as I name them. I skip this with the fastest children. Then I shuffle the words and show them one at a time, as the child reads them to me. Sometimes the child plays teacher (especially if the child has little power at home) and the game is that I make a lot of errors for my teacher to correct. Then we work on a book if one's ready, or discuss the last one that went home: "What room is it in? Who likes to hear you read it? Who else? Are they proud of your reading?"

If Leslie knows her old words well, we cooperatively find a new one, and I shuffle it into a dozen of her old words. Showing her each word in turn, I ask "Is this 'grandma'?" and require a complete, formal answer, "No, it's 'Harry' " or "Yes, it's 'grandma'." Next I ask Leslie if she wants to write today. If not, her lesson is over. If she does, I give her her name, and then ask if she wants more. She can choose additional words from her envelope to write. Some fours will be comfortable tracing as many as three or four words at a sitting. After that they can learn to copy your writing just below your model on the page. Encourage the children to write as big as you do. Don't hurry to get to the copying stage: it means failure for some children of this age. Be conservative about this!

By spring I ask the children, "Do you want a little writing or a lot?" Then I give those who want a little just their names, and the others get a three or four word sentence. Watching the children's real pride in reading and writing is one of the great joys I've known as a teacher.

I've described an optimum situation for teaching reading: Katherine and the group out in the yard, me alone with a child just inside the classroom. This works best. I've also taught reading at the park, carrying cards, markers, and envelopes in an old tote and working with one child on the bench while the others played on the equipment. If the situation had become still harder, I'd have continued with some of the children: the satisfaction I get from teaching reading makes it possible to bear some of the hard things about teaching in difficult situations, so I can't imagine giving it up.

In early May we show the parents how to teach their children reading. At graduation we give the parents a complete set of materials for this kind of reading instruction: a marking pen, a deck of blank cards, their child's old words, and the envelope. Some parents continue to instruct their children, and some don't, but the continuity is possible, and I get satisfaction from the demystification it implies.

Encouraging parents to teach reading to their children was not fashionable when I first began to teach. In fact, when I took the test to teach in New York City in 1962, there was a question that went: "Of the following books that might be in a child's desk, which one should not be permitted to go home overnight with the child?" The correct answer was the Reader. Their reasoning was that if a child got ahead of the reading group, his or her interest level would be lowered. And if you lower normal motivation to read a Reader, then there isn't any motivation left.

Amidst all the discussions about why children fail to learn to read, one reason seems clear to me. Children don't learn to read at school if adults don't take responsibility for teaching them. Teachers reliably go through whatever processes they think are required, and the children who can learn to read that way do so. The rest have been taught, but they don't know how to read. Only children identified as failures normally get the one-to-one attention that we take as central to our program. Even remedial reading is rarely tailored to the individual child's tastes, style, and interests.

Our way gives the children a great deal of control over the process. The vocabulary means a lot to them, they are in charge and interested, and when we have picked a wrong word, we throw it out again. This is consistent with their developmental needs, so it works and they read—not only Ivan and Amanda, but Millie and Lukash as well.

Perspective
Evaluating teachers fairly

What was a Heffalump like?
Was it Fierce?
Did it come when you whistled? And how did it come?
Was it Fond of Pigs at all?
If it was Fond of Pigs, did it make any difference what sort of Pig?
Supposing it was Fierce with Pigs, would it make any difference if the Pig had a grandfather called TRESPASSERS WILLIAM?

—Winnie-the-Pooh

Most of this book is about how to teach amid the real problems we all know exist in the schools. In this chapter and the final chapter of the book I'm going to talk about things that could make the schools better.

Even in ideal circumstances teaching calls for a wide range of gifts. Instead, we have in the schools many teachers whose gifts are underdeveloped, and others who, having chosen teaching for its security or respectability, show little interest in finding new solutions when old ones fail.

The worst of these teachers are not evaluated, and the best of them find no support. Neither is held to any clear standards except those they impose on themselves. When I promote Amanda, who feels good about herself, to a teacher who tells her for a whole year that she isn't special or smart, then I want to see that teacher evaluated and removed, so he can't do any more damage.

Administrators wring their hands. "There's nothing we can do. The unions won't stand for evaluation." The unions reply, "We believe in evaluation, but these administrators are subjective and careless of the due process to which our members are entitled." In effect, these two powerful groups are in collusion to keep our clients, the children and parents, from getting the best service.

Their objections can be met in at least a dozen ways. Let me tell you about one I've worked with for eight years. The Child Development Associate credential was established for upgrading Head Start personnel, but it embodies an idea that could be used anywhere. It is competency-based, field-based, and criterion-referenced. Here is the definition of a CDA:

The Child Development Associate or CDA is a person able to meet the specific needs of children and who, with parents and other adults, works to nurture children's physical, social, emotional and intellectual growth in a child development framework. The CDA conducts herself or himself in an ethical manner.

You can earn your credential in as little as three months, or as long as it takes. You may be a teacher or a paraprofessional, have a degree or be a high-school dropout. The credential is equivalent to an A.A. degree in some states, and can be worth up to 30 credits at one college in California.

My friend Yuko Marshall got her CDA credential recently. Here's what happened.

First, Yuko applied to the CDA National Credentialing Office in Washington, D.C. She sent in the papers and money throughout the process, and I won't go into that here, since that sort of thing is apt to change. Next she selected two members for her Local Assessment Team: Gigi Gregory, a parent who had had a child in Yuko's class a couple of years back, and me, a friend with early childhood training. She made sure that her supervisor at work, Kate Rosen, was comfortable with the idea of her undertaking the process. Then she began to crack the CDA code, and to learn their way of dividing experience into manageable bits.

The National Credentialing office sent materials intended to help the candidate succeed, including examples of good practices and definitions of the thirteen functional areas in which she would be evaluated. Here are two definitions so you get the idea:

"Communication—Candidate provides opportunities for children to understand, acquire, and use verbal and nonverbal means of communicating thoughts and feelings."

"Self—Candidate helps each child to know, accept, and take pride in himself or herself and to develop a sense of independence."

Yuko needed to understand the definitions of the areas, and then to assess her competence in each one. My job was to help her look at her skills and to suggest strategies for strengthening them as needed. I was responsible for observing her teaching at least three times, at least three weeks apart. I wrote a record of each visit, giving examples of her work in each of the thirteen areas.

Gigi got the parents to fill out questionnaires and summarized them. She observed Yuko's teaching for three hours, recording what she saw in each functional area.

Yuko prepared a portfolio, with at least three exhibits in each area, showing what she understood and practiced. She took photographs of children at work, included things the children had made, and wrote commentaries expressing her attitudes and policies.

When all of us had done our work, Yuko sent a readiness form to Washington, and after a while Maritza Macdonald called Yuko, Gigi, and me to say she was our CDA Representative, and to arrange an afternoon for the four of us to meet as Yuko's Local Assessment Team.

Maritza observed Yuko teach that morning, interviewed Yuko at noontime, and brought to the meeting her written observations of Yuko's work. After we had read each other's materials, we discussed each functional area in turn. Our judgment of her performance and our recommendations for her continuing growth were entered on a profile, one copy of which remained with Yuko. The rest of the documentation went to Washington.

At the meeting's end, we enthusiastically voted 4-0 to award Yuko the CDA Credential. The final vote must be unanimous for the credential to be awarded.

Considering the CDA as a model for assessing teachers and encouraging ongoing development among them, what are its advantages?

• This kind of process provides a kind but exacting climate for teachers to grow in. Such growth cannot be rooted in an adversary relationship.

• In the process of learning what the structure is about, the candidate reviews and clarifies her work. Yuko says that the most important thing for her was learning the reasons behind what she teaches.

• In the CDA model Yuko paces her own assessment. She invites into it two of her three evaluators based on some sort of harmony she feels with those people, and thus has friends around her during the team meeting.

• There is due process. Yuko doesn't feel like a victim, as she might in the sort of evaluation where the boss observes and writes what suits his or her fancy.

• An incompetent candidate can't easily yell "unfair" when his or her unacceptable performance is documented by a team.

• The documentation is drawn from five observations (of varied styles, by three people on at least five different days) as well as the perceptions of the parents whose children the candidate is teaching. This split screen permits a clearer view than any one evaluator could bring to the process. The diversity of views increases the reliability of the outcome and the likelihood that children will get good teachers.

• The structure is clear and exemplifies principles of positive interaction between teacher and child, teacher and colleague, teacher and community.

Good programs for children require quality control. Knowing that the CDA works encourages me to dream of a rational teacher training structure, of schools which base perquisites on demonstrated skills rather than whim, and of getting rid of teachers who don't want to work and grow.

Unions and administrators must make room for fair assessment, or else parents and community leaders must throw the rascals out.

III

The Rhythm
of the
Year

I've come to see the school year as a cycle of seasons. In summer the teacher recharges energy and plans for the coming year. In autumn she or he studies the children's skills and their parents' values, and teaches the children routines which help them to find independence. In the winter he or she teaches in order to augment children's skills and confidence. And in the spring the teacher, children, and parents celebrate the achievements of the year.

Working for a number of years with four-year-olds from the same community made me surer about some techniques as they succeeded year after year, and persuaded me that others simply didn't work for me. I often railed at the artificiality of the nine-month relationship I had with these children, wishing that I could keep them for a couple of years and see them continue to grow. But whatever the drawbacks of having the same assignment for seven years, the chance to see the year unfold was there, and it has colored all my perceptions of teaching.

1

"Mary will come back to school on Thursday": The intake interview

"Rabbit," said Pooh to himself. "I <u>*like*</u> *talking to Rabbit. He talks about sensible things. He doesn't use long, difficult words, like Owl. He uses short, easy words like 'What about lunch?' and 'Help yourself, Pooh.' . . ."*

—The House at Pooh Corner

Interviewing a parent at the beginning of the school year is a strain on both of us. Often a parent is concerned about doing things right, how her or his child will be judged, and how to present the family to the school. Parents may be worried about links between the school and other institutions with which they deal: Department of Social Services, medical institutions, Food Stamps, adoption, foster care, police, probation office, and all the rest.

I too want to do things right. I hope to calm the fear and anger the parent may have toward schools, teachers, and authority figures in general. I want to achieve a collaboration in which each of us can trust that we both have the child's interest at heart. At the interview I try to convey the notion that since the institutional system oppresses both of us, we have to work together to fight it, and especially the School District, on behalf of the child.

Unwittingly, the School District helps us a lot with this introduction, by giving us a quantity of paper forms. To fill in the blanks, a mother may need to state for the record that she lives alone with her children. But if the child is going to talk to us about a daddy, we need to know that he exists. So I ask her, "Just for my information, who are all the people who live in your house? I'm not going to put your business in the street, but to be a good teacher to your child, I have to know what's going on."

If this works, the parent shares some kinds of information with me as a representative of an institution, and other information with me as an ally up against that same institution. It's a peculiar event. Given the threatening nature of the school system, I feel that this is a positive way for school-home connections to begin, with parent and teacher supporting or defending the children against the depredations of a large, unfeeling school district.

I tell the parent that we discuss in class how we want our school to be. We talk with children in the group about whether we want a safe school or a scary school, and we come back to that discussion again and again. On occasion a child may say "I want a scary school," just to see what will happen. Generally, I respond to this by standing up and being a monster and saying "Aaaargh" a little too close to that child. I'm so menacing that the child is scared. Then I ask quietly "Do you really want a scary school?" and the little voice says "No." Once we get our terms defined, we can agree to keep the school safe.

On those occasions when the school has been burglarized, we've discussed the theft at circle time. The children are concerned and angry, and offer to help. They offer their dog to get the crook, or promise to beat him up or to get their brother-father-uncle-friend to beat him up. Having contracted for safe space, they are furious to find out that not everyone honors that agreement. If you're willing to give up being bad in a space, you naturally expect everybody else to do likewise. A week after one theft, Wesley told Katherine he was scared that the man who robbed the school would come back and beat us up. Wesley said he was going to fight him—and wanted to know if the grownups would stay and help. We told him we knew it was scary, and we were glad he loved his school, but that grownups, not children, deal with robbers.

Whenever we adults feel that the degree of safety in the school is eroding, we go back to this subject with the children. They are sensible about wanting the school nice and safe, and tell each other how that can be brought about. I've never seen this discussion fail to rouse the preacher in a couple of children, and the peer exhortation works.

During the intake interview we discuss children's anger and ways they express it. I start by asking what sorts of things make this child angry: not getting her or his own way? not wanting to share? not being allowed to go somewhere? After the parent has told me something about the child's style of anger, I say I feel that children this age need something that is okay to do when they're angry, something physical, rough, permitted. In our classroom we let children hit a pillow and kick it if they're angry, or even if they just want to. I suggest that at home it might be okay to hit the bed or rip up old newspapers. We grownups have a lot of acceptable things we do when angry: go for a walk, get drunk, slam the door, etc. It seems that people who don't express their anger grow ulcers and other ills instead.

Often a little child who has discharged some anger by hitting and kicking an uncaring object is ready to do some rational work on the problem. Anger, until released, gets in the way of the work. Parents respond positively to this information, because they really want to support their children. They say "I think my child would like that," or "I never thought of that. I'll give it a try."

Parents sometimes ask how we discipline children, and I tell them about benching. If a child hits another, the hitter sits down for a period of time. The duration of benching is sometimes determined by the victim, because we feel that when the victim is ready to let the assailant up, the issue is really ended.

One great thing about working with kids is that even when you are at your wits' end, they are resourceful. I enjoy telling parents about an occasion when things weren't working well, the children weren't listening to me, and I was beside myself, ready to explode. Finally I sat down on our rug and, projecting my voice grandly, said: "I don't like the way things are going around here and I'm tired of being a yelling teacher, and I'm going to sit down and not do anything, and I don't even feel like being the grownup and taking care of you, so you'd better make me feel better 'cause you made me feel cranky." There was a tremendous, long silence.

Then Bernice, skinniest and least verbal of children, looked at me, raised an eyebrow, and said in her thin little voice, "Happy Birthday?" I responded gruffly: "You gonna sing 'Happy Birthday'? Think that'll make me feel better?" "Uh huh." "Well, try it. It might work." And they did.

They sang me that best, happiest song. They lifted their voices and carolled to me, and by the time they were halfway through I was grinning. It seemed true wisdom on Bernice's part to find a way to soothe me. I really had no idea what would happen when I challenged the children, but I know I couldn't have accomplished what they did.

I tell parents that we value choosing as an activity. We think it helps children grow if they make choices and live with the results. The children respect the school for letting them make decisions. I explain that we teach them that if they want something to take home, they have to make it. This kind of planning takes sophistication, and isn't obvious to many fours.

At the intake interview we discuss the problem of double jeopardy. I explain that if we report a child's misbehavior at school, she or he will already have been punished: put on the bench or not allowed back on the bike for the rest of the day. I say I don't want parents to punish the child again, and that I won't punish for what was done wrong at home. If they do punish the child for problems at school, I'll want to stop sharing what's happening. That's not a good way for adults who care about a child to work together.

Sometimes a child says to me "Don't tell my mama." I usually ask why. And the child might say "She'll spank me." So, if I really have to tell mama about wet pants or a bloody nose, I make a contract with the child. "If I tell your mama, I'll make sure she knows you don't need a spanking." Most parents recognize this as fair play.

Parent, child, and I all have to work on trust in our relationship, and that's always hard to do, especially with an institution looming over us to shadow our values. I resent how badly the parents were treated in their own schooling; their memories make it hard for them to trust me, given my color and my job title.

The intake interview is a good place to make parents' expectations of us fit our own. I warn parents that I'm very hard on people who pick up their children late. I ask that they tell whoever comes for their child to be on time.

Usually Katherine plays with the child while I interview the parent. When the papers are filled out and the discussion is over, I pay some attention to the child, asking about what she or he was doing while mama or daddy and I talked, admiring the drawing or the putting away of ladder blocks or whatever. This gives me a quick sense of the child's comfort with language in a strange environment, and the distance the child permits the parent.

When I feel that a child is going to have difficulty letting the parent go, or if I haven't met the child before the start of school, I tell the parent that on the first days parents may either stay or go. When they leave they should tell their children "I'll be back." What they may not do is teeter on the doorstep, or sneak away. Even if the child breaks into tears, parents who have said goodbye must keep going, saying by this action: "I trust these grownups to take care of you." If parents don't trust us, they should hang around until they do!

I promise that I will hold and comfort a child who cries, and that toys and other children usually draw a crying child into play. If after a week, the child still cries when the parent leaves, I suggest that a toy or blanket from home may help give a feeling of continuity. I also encourage parents to make clear their expectations every day, on the trip to school, telling the child, "Soon you will be able to say goodbye without crying. You know I'll come to get you later."

After parent and child leave the intake interview, Katherine and I compare our experience of them. She reports to me on child style and competence, and I report to her on parent style and disclosure. We enter this kind of material in our logbook, because if we don't, these new people tend to blur into each other and precious clues to teaching get lost. Since I can't keep track of people until I know them a little, I prefer fall registration to spring registration. Also, in the fall I can assure Mary that she'll be back soon, but in the spring I must resort to things like "You'll come back to school in a long, long time, when the big kids go to school, too." I'm not satisfied with that. It leaves me hanging. In the fall I give a child a note to take home. It says "Mary will come back to school on Thursday," and the children seem to understand that the piece of paper is a promise.

2

A view from the treehouse:
On room arrangement

There are people who begin the Zoo at the beginning, called WAYIN, and walk as quickly as they can past every cage until they get to the one called WAYOUT, but the nicest people go straight to the animal they love most, and stay there.

—Winnie-the-Pooh

Before going to school, children learn whatever they pick up from their surroundings, and they make very interesting choices. These add up to a personal style. School gives many children their first experience of learning with an explicit objective. Since it's necessary to all learning, we show them how to channel their attention to what they're trying to learn.

Keeping the visual field uncluttered helps children focus on the material they're using. When we want a child to look at something, we isolate it on an empty table or a blank wall. I teach reading with my back to a wall, so that nothing interesting happens behind me to distract the children. I read stories in a corner so latecomers arrive at the back of the group. This saves me large amounts of energy each day.

The children learn to screen out each other's play. This is easy when you're doing something comfortable, but much harder when you're working on something new and difficult. The number of activities that can coexist pleasantly depends on how space is utilized. At 8:52 on a typical October morning we had two boys building with Free Form Posts, two boys "cooking" in the doll corner, two boys drawing with a volunteer at a table, two girls eating at the snack table, one boy throwing beanbags into a board with cutouts, a boy pushing a doll carriage, a boy watching a visiting guinea pig, two girls arguing over who will read a book first, and two boys arriving. Three children were absent.

Unless care is taken, accidents of space will determine your program. Like most nursery schools, we meet in a circle every day for singing, discussions, and other group lessons. After many years I moved the circle from an area near the door to another, quite far away, so that parents can come in without children noticing them. This gives parents a much more realistic sense of what we're

87

doing. If the room hadn't been so clearly designed to have the circle in the corner near the door, I might have thought of it years sooner.

The architect who designed our kindergarten wing put no bulletin boards or chalk boards at child eye level, but built permanent shelves just where those boards should go. All the cabinets were designed for adults, with the top shelves much too high for children to use. The room was disguised to look as if thought about children went into it, but no one who respects children could possibly have approved those blueprints.

We created far more child-oriented space in an ancient storefront in Harlem, by rebuilding in Tri-wall cardboard, with all the adult furnishings up high, so the children could have all the low space. We used many nesting arrangements, so that things that were not in use were tucked away.

In larger classrooms, you can have areas which serve only one purpose, like the tiling area we left up at Burnett for several weeks, or a table devoted to cornstarch and water.

The way classroom space is divided and activities are choreographed makes a big difference in how well teachers and children are able to focus on their tasks. We encourage different kinds of play by dividing the room into areas: a doll-house and a treehouse; a block-building space; a story corner; a waterplay area; a place for the easel, clay crock, glue, markers and such; and a place for meetings, dancing, and music. Our climbing dome lets the children do something physical indoors. We also have a valuable area that can be darkened for play around themes of night and dreaming.

Two adults who share a classroom can use opposite corners, each taking part of the group. Katherine works more patiently than I with less articulate children, so she does simple games which teach basic vocabulary. In the opposite corner I build charts or tell stories with the chattier children.

The dollhouse is the children's space. Adults go into it only if invited. I may stop by for a cup of "coffee," but I rarely hang out in the house because I'm too big and my presence seems to redirect or inhibit the play. We supply the house with empty cans and boxes of wholesome foods, with hats and vests and radios and dark glasses and ice-cube trays: anything that encourages complex language and play.

We limit the doll corner to six children, the climbing dome to four, and the treehouse to two. There are pictographs posted to remind the children of these limits. The dome is a favorite spot for children—some relax there after small muscle work by swinging or climbing on it, while others scramble up and perch on the top, watching all the bustle of our room. From the log:

Yesterday I taught a big lesson on limiting the dome to four children. Today Leslie walked over, counted 1, 2, 3, and then climbed on!

We enforce treehouse rules strictly, because it's high and I'm frightened by daredevil behavior. We keep books and teddy bears and pillows there, and a pulley "elevator" brings up other toys and books, and takes them down again later, so the children's hands are free for climbing. The pulley comes down each June, and goes back up in October, after the new children have learned to go up and down holding on with both hands. Careful selection of materials helps make the day flow and keeps the atmosphere pleasant. Our three rules for buying materials are: 1) Choose materials which do what they're supposed to do and won't self-destruct when children use them. 2) Buy enough of each material to minimize competition and long waiting for turns. I'd much rather have enough Lego for six children than one childs-worth each of six construction toys. 3) The most important rule is that our books and materials must reflect the ethnic heritage of the children. There must be appropriate food and clothing in the house. We avoid materials that stereotype roles (doctor kits featuring boys on the package or jewelry with only girl models) as we offer girls and boys equal opportunity for development.

Each game needs its own place and appropriate container. We can only insist that children replace materials if there are clear places for them.

We've found that two double easels stay busy in a group of 15 to 20 four-year-olds. We give the children red, blue, yellow, black and white paint, and help them mix other colors when they ask for them. Our clay crock is plastic, with a tight-sealing lid, and keeps grapefruit-sized balls of clay moist. Children remove a ball of clay from the crock, taking it and a washable masonite board to a nearby table. When done they remake the ball and return the clay to the crock, except for the rare and wonderful occasion when Lukash makes a magical face of clay and wants to keep it, or Leslie makes a wonderful animal that stands on its own feet.

Like any place people live in, the classroom needs cozy and spacious areas, soft and hard ones, spaces devoted to particular activity and others that change with the shifting interests of the children. The physical room both reflects and determines the program. Like the program, it warrants regular reassessment and redesign. The best use of space will result in a classroom which invites children to experiment and discover and relax.

3

Getting started:
The first day of school

"There's a thing called Twy-stymes," he said. "Christopher Robin tried to teach it to me once, but it didn't."
"What didn't?" said Rabbit.
"Didn't what?" said Piglet.
Pooh shook his head.
"I don't know," he said. "It just didn't."

—The House at Pooh Corner

We always spend hours planning the first day of school. We keep it short, with just a few children at a time. We offer toys and activities that are attractive, simple, and easy to complete. We begin teaching children's and teachers' names.

Some of our children arrive expecting incoherence and disorganization in people and things. Some have been punished for being curious and exploring. From the first day we seek to teach them how to trust. We make promises and keep them. We make mistakes and acknowledge them. We hope to reestablish trial and error as a basic and reasonable process.

If the enrollment is large, we may have three "first days" rather than admit more than six or seven children at a time. Children come for just an hour and a half a day for three or four days, then start to come for the full session. Those who begin later in the year start by coming to our last hour for a few days. This is kinder than having them come early and making them leave just when an interesting activity begins. The later in the year a child joins us, the more we ask other children to teach the newcomer.

One year our first day's program was:

1. Saying hello to the teachers.
2. Looking at the flower of the day.
3. Saying goodbye to Mama or Daddy.
4. Putting wraps away in a cubby marked with the child's name.
5. Examining the room and choosing a toy.

6. Locating the toilets and learning to climb the treehouse, supervised by Katherine or me.
7. Eating a snack.
8. Going outdoors to ride bikes and take Polaroid pictures.
9. Hearing a story.
10. Going home.

Our greeting is personal, up close, with eyes level. We cross the room to greet a child, and together with Mama or Daddy we look at the flower, which is at child's eye level.

To stop at the door and talk with a teacher about a flower seems a good way to focus the children on school. As the year goes on, we ask more and more of this early-morning encounter. Our demand that the child talk is balanced by the attention and beauty we offer. If children can't remember a flower's name after a reasonable period, we ask them to find out from others nearby. In a year we may have marigolds, fuschias, geraniums, chrysanthemums, impatiens and daffodils. Marigolds are great, because we can take apart the old flowers, which are composed of seeds, then plant the seeds and grow more flowers, all in a two-month cycle.

For the first day's activities the children choose from any materials on display. We offer only attractive materials which promise a high probability of success.

Ivan listened to the story tape eagerly, later telling his foster mother, "It says 'Turn the page, the cow jump over the moon.' "

Hamid painted twice and was very quiet and self-contained. He was anxious when he tried the tree puzzle, and uncomfortable both on the dome and up in the treehouse.

Kathye chose a three piece puzzle and then kept her fingers around the pieces so they couldn't fit into the places. When she painted she put her brush down, then slowly and with purpose put both hands palms down against the paint, held them a few seconds, took them away, and watched closely for our reaction. We showed her how to wash off the paint at the sink. We made a note to give her fingerpaint soon. She dimpled and beamed as she played with the water.

Playing with a tray full of seashells, Leslie arranged a surprisingly methodical border of shells all around the tray. Other children chose building with one-inch cubes, drawing with markers, and building with the ladder blocks they had played with on registration day.

During the play period we peel the children away from work for a few minutes, one or two at a time, to show them the toilets and teach them how to climb up the treehouse. This prevents accidents in the two most likely places, and gives each child a direct experience of learning from Katherine or me. As we ask the children to leave their work we promise "You'll be back soon to finish up." This is the first promise we tell the children. We keep it, and thus begin to build trust.

We note any difficulty in climbing. We inspect shoes, telling parents if they're not safe. From our first day's log:

Leslie liked going up to the top of the treehouse and calling down "Hi!"
Lukash's grubby face lit up when he looked down at us from up so high.
Daphne proudly showed Kathye how to flush the toilets.

On the first day we serve a very simple snack, trying to be as peaceful as possible about it. Lots of theory about eating may be on our minds, but we keep the food experience familiar and pleasant from the start. Children may eat at the table or in the yard, as they prefer.

Outdoors, Ivan could hardly wait till his Polaroid picture developed. He helped me count to sixty, only needing help with the tens, then grinned at his picture, which showed him, gap-toothed, smiling.

By the time I asked the kids to go indoors, they were ready to leave the beloved bikes to see what came next. Kathye got to the rug first, and I asked her to look at a book until the others were ready. She burst into tears, looked at me for sympathy and then went and got a book as if it had been her own idea! When the meeting began, she beamed her moonfaced smile through the singing and talking, although the story didn't engage her and she wiggled a good bit.

For the first day I pick a story with a chorus, *Goodnight Moon* by Margaret Wise Brown, or, some years, if the group is very talky, *Caps For Sale* by Esphyr Slobodkina. Some time is given to settling children on the rug so they can all see the pictures. After we have eliminated legitimate reasons for commotion, Katherine and I are both quite dramatic in our hushing when somebody inter-rupts. We encourage the children to chorus the repetitive parts of the story, and praise them for catching on.

If the day has been suitably paced, parents come in during the story and are ready to take children home at its end. We dismiss children individually, and by name, to show respect, to know who's left, and to make sure parents get mes-sages and other material. We try to tell each parent something accurate, pleas-ant, and individual about the child's day. When the group is very small and we aren't rushed, sometime in the day we take a few minutes with each child to write a note that tells parents what we did and is presented to parents at dismissal. After a very full hour-and-a-half, everyone was dismissed but Leslie, who was very worried because her mother wasn't there to pick her up. Arriving 15 min-utes later, Mama was deeply apologetic and promised her child she'd be on time in the future.

We ask children to do what they can by themselves, but we try to shelter them if they feel strange and lonely. When Kathye finishes with a toy, she must put it back. If she needs a grownup to help, she gets one. But she does a share of her work herself, since the community pattern in the school demands that from the first day on.

What we're leading up to with this demand is reflected in a log from May. It's about my own daughter, Jenny, who one day spent 35 minutes examining her shoe and taking out a shoelace, then asked me to put it back in. I told her if she wanted to take them out, she should put them back in. She did.

4

Helping teachers grow: Logging

Pooh went into a corner and tried saying 'Aha!' in that sort of a voice. Sometimes it seemed to him that it did mean what Rabbit said, and sometimes it seemed to him that it didn't. "I suppose it's just practice," he thought. "I wonder if Kanga will have to practice too so as to understand it."

—Winnie-the-Pooh

Before each school year I have nightmares. I dream I don't know how to handle the new children and the classroom becomes a shambles. After twenty-odd years of teaching, I still can't assume that the old solutions will work with new children. Teaching people, changing their minds, can't be done lightly or casually. Try to remember the best solution you have yet found to a given problem, use it again, and see if it still works. If it doesn't, observe the problem and revise the best solution so it's better yet. Let's stop pretending we have answers when we don't. Many times we don't understand what children are doing. From the log:

March 1: Willie seems to get a thrill every time someone is hurt. Also, when you tell a group of children something, Willie doesn't act like he was included.

We don't know what this means when isolated. But we have noted it, and when we know more about Willie's cruelty and kindness we will make a plan. Likewise, when we address a group of which he's a part we'll take pains to look directly at him, including him in the collective "you." Six days later: Thomas fell and Willie took care of him. Later Willie fell and Thomas cared for him!

Four days after that: Thomas is overmuch into wrestling—gets scared in the middle and doesn't know what to do. This is also true of Willie. Adults have to keep firmer hold on the "ding" and rescue these children. We'll try offering the wrestlers one ding per match . . . a child's "ding" ends his or her wrestling for the day.

Two weeks later: Willie is moving into a stage of more awareness of destructive activity, of hitting and hurting. He's taking a little care of his clothing. Ron thinks he's interested in finding acceptable behavior at school!

And, during the following week: Willie complained repeatedly to Ron that somebody did something or other to somebody or other. Then he waited to hear if it was okay or not. Willie did two hard puzzles. Seems a little surprised when he's successful. Getting hooked on competence.

Looking for a better way is the goal of our logging process. We report what has worked and share ideas about what might work. Then we come back to record what happened and our conjectures about why. We always have to act on too little information, but at least the information is collected methodically every day. We try to stay flexible in the face of our fantasy as to who the child is, reversing and turning corners as new data come in. To refine the guessing mechanism through logging makes a good teacher better.

Unfortunately, we all tend to stereotype the people we meet, deciding they're like other people we've known and projecting qualities and foibles of these others onto them. Settling for stereotypes can make teachers miss the essence of a child. We collect oddments in the log:

Millie won't say goodbye when she leaves.

Hal "can't find his stuff" at dismissal.

Willie gets worried and puts his finger in his mouth when the first parents arrive. Awaits his tardy brother anxiously.

Thomas on list to hammer but never got a turn. I promised he will tomorrow. Promise is posted at workbench.

Shabazz said, "I have a mommy and a daddy and I live with them and you can't put me in your puppet show." I asked him to come talk with me. "Do you know what a puppet show is?" He nodded. "Is it scary?" No answer. "When I was a little girl I used to be scared of puppets, but then I found out they were just dolls, and people make them talk in funny voices. You're very strong, and you're in charge of the puppet and you can make the puppet do whatever you want it to. That's called a puppet show. If you get scared, come running to me and I'll tell you again how you're in charge." Shabazz played puppet show for half an hour after that.

The best way to grow as a teacher is to study something interesting to you that is far removed from your usual teaching, like gardening, pantomime, juggling, massage, or belly dance. Watch yourself as you learn something new and hard, and you'll find out more about learning and teaching. Once you have a handle on the new subject, you can teach it to the children, if it's appropriate. As a grown teacher, you can teach anything you understand to almost anyone. You analyze the components of the thing to be learned, and combine that with your understanding of how you came to know it.

The narrowest approach is only to teach subjects you were taught in teacher training college; simplistic, factual, rote information everybody "knows" belongs in schools. The opposite is to teach what you are, to expose your process to the children so they can begin to see how you make your choices.

As I become more experienced, I develop habitual ways of solving certain kinds of problems. When a solution doesn't work, I try to redefine the problem and modify the habit. Some solutions never quite fit the problem. Periodically I take out my problem-solving habits and examine them, replacing buttons, letting down hems, giving away ones that don't fit the person I've become, and searching for new ones that do fit. For instance, trying to get children to use their right and left hands correctly in the *Hokey Pokey*, I used to put them in a line so that all the lefts would be "toward the window" and all the rights "toward the cubbies." Since this never really worked, I hit upon writing with chalk on the right hand, and doing exercises all day that referred to the right and left hands, having children look for the chalk to remember which is the right one.

I love to have colleagues, student teachers, administrators, parents and friends come to observe, because their impressions inform what I'm doing. For years I've told everyone who wanted to visit to come ahead, but that they'd have to stay and log the session with us, as compost for our garden. Visiting adults who comment on what we're doing give me a lift. Often their insights start me thinking about a child in a way that really helps.

At the beginning of the year we log each child each day. Later on we log only significant behavior. What we log depends on what has happened that day. If we are concerned about Ivan and have agreed to discuss him in depth, we summarize our observations of his day. Another day's log might describe an activity which caught the imagination of the group. Clues to children's styles often emerge from first times: first trip to the park, who held back and who jumped right in, first fingerpainting, who was afraid of the messiness and who wallowed in it, and so on.

It takes time and discipline to log each day, and many of the people who have worked with us have resisted logging. Teachers discover after about three months, however, that having specific data to return to makes them more sensitive to the children.

Without a log one doesn't remember the initial shyness, inarticulateness, and inability to drive a trike. The gains that are made aren't reflected to the teacher in a tangible way. When you write down what's going on, you improve the likelihood that you will recognize growth when it occurs. The recognition that your work is taking hold is a high motivation to teach some more.

If this book causes you to try logging for three months I'll be delighted. What's more, your kids will change more rapidly, and so will your pride in your work. Please write to me in care of the publisher about your experiences with keeping a log.

Observations and diagnoses lead to prescriptions based on what we've been able to understand about the children so far. The changes we observe are sometimes so rapid that it seems dangerous to say anything except "This is what I saw today." This way we make all the judgments we like, but only for the moment, always expecting the children to change.

When a child seems to have changed style, we check the logbook to see if we can find any clues that might explain why. I make a point of reading the log during both long vacations, and plan for the next season based on what I find there.

Of course, when we make referrals to doctors or therapists, we send them large chunks of the logbook. When Andy's parents complained of his "effeminacy" and asked us to help with a referral, we sent the psychologist the following excerpts:

January 8: Admitted to prekindergarten. No previous schooling. Seems tense. Asked to play with water and had to be told four times that it's to be kept in the sink. Doesn't coordinate two hands, unable to open plastic box. Sweet. Quiet. Played 45 minutes with dolls and doll clothing alongside P (a boy.) Climbed up to treehouse and down again very well.

January 12: Built with Lincoln Logs, "washed dishes," drew (sexual interest apparent—his people look like penises). Continues quiet, graceful, interested in doll play, and unsure of his next move if it involves others. On his own he's quite self-possessed. Knows (and shows off) colors and shapes.

January 18: Played with D, M, and T (all boys). M told him "You must be a girl cause you play with dolls." This didn't seem to faze him.

January 23: Showed tentative aggressive behavior toward H on the playground. Gave him a small push. Seems to think he can sing without articulating words.

January 26: Cried because he wanted to climb on the dome and it was full. Ron observed "He cries like a kid who's not supposed to cry." Trouble with P over sharing firehats.

February 7: Constantly in dollhouse, cooking and dressing up. Today he flounced around, pranced, and looked at Ron for a reaction; Ron put on a shawl and joined him in his dance.

February 16: Didn't want to take his collage or his painting home. Wore high heels most of the morning.

February 19: Watched Susan as she hammered. Cried inappropriately much when he fell on the playground.

February 22: Can really run in high heels! Used Cuisenaire rods to make alphabet letters.

February 26: Got very involved wrestling with T. Enjoyed singing and dancing with other children.

February 28: Didn't want Susan to be the mother in the house. Sawed with Ron.

March 1: I found him weeping in the house. Told me "Nobody wants to play with me." I asked whom he wanted, and he named Susan—just then she walked in, looking for him. I told her he was lonely and she slipped an arm around him and said, "I'll take care of you."

March 10: Told us he is six years old. (His sister is six, he's four. We're beginning to think some of his sex-role confusion is because he identifies with her. Maybe.)

March 16: Says his stepdaddy hollered at him, "and my mommy told him to get out and my real daddy Andy's in the house. Stepdaddy likes my sister, but mama likes me."

March 17: Immediately noticed Sondra's minor haircut.

March 29: Has been in school since January 8. Reads his own name, sister's name, "man," "dress," "up," "cry," and "Butch."

From our report to the psychologist:

We conferred with Andy's mother and stepfather, urging less pressure on him. His father came to school complaining of the play curriculum, but was mollified to see his son read and do arithmetic. He seems to be very concerned with Andy's upbringing to date; Andy spent two years with a grandmother "down south" and the father blames her for Andy's role confusion. Father blusters that he will take over the child if things don't improve fast.

Andy's mother says nothing specific about either of her children or their play. She generalizes: "He's a mama's boy," or "Carrie's the rough one." She says Andy keeps up with Carrie, and occasionally beats her up. Despite two years' age difference, they're about the same size. Mother defers to her two husbands and their opinions, presenting no "fight" on behalf of her son.

We see Andy copying the female models he admires, and very afraid of the men in his life, both of whom are very very big and loud. We see him lacking support in the family, and very much in need of peaceful acceptance.

As with most of our children, we didn't see how Andy turned out, because he moved back south. Since we don't read the final chapters, we'd better be sure we've done what we can for the Andys. That's the satisfaction we get.

We keep many, many records of children's activity because they move in such varied rhythms, and we want to make intelligent choices about intervening. There are some activities we want all the children to try six or eight times. By then they have enough information to make a sensible decision about whether they enjoy them.

So I say to a wandering child, "I don't think you've played with clay for a long while, so I want you to put on an apron and get out some clay." I check off the puzzles, which we keep in the right order to ensure continued success. A child who hasn't yet learned about using blocks is asked once a week to build, usually with someone who likes blocks and uses them well. When children say "I don't want to," we answer, "Sometimes you choose what you're going to do, and sometimes I do." Most see this as fair. An outdoorsy child who has still not sewn for more than a couple of minutes is given sewing. By the way, those styrofoam trays under meat and fish in supermarkets make wonderful sewing materials. We give the children real needles and thread, doubling the thread and knotting it so the needle won't get lost, and putting the needle through the tray. If they prick a finger, we say seriously, "Put your finger in your mouth."

Our record-keeping allows children to move through activities at their own pace, without missing what we adults like to think are the most basic experiences: painting, modelling clay, block-building; tricycling, skating and climbing; listening to story tapes and dictating stories and reading; counting and sorting and playing with number materials; dancing, singing and playing instruments. Children who do many things quickly and easily have more time left than those who learn at a slower pace. A child who chooses to paint will not be asked to paint by the adults. One who never volunteers will be sent to the easel about once a week. We consider painting important for the way it lets children watch themselves grow and change.

Leslie started by painting the same picture over and over. It was discrete patches of the five colors we give out and always the same sequence of colors. When you put two or three of her paintings together, it was perfectly clear that all were by the same artist. In late October Leslie branched out. She filled up the page with color, she let colors touch each other, she painted one color over another, and she discovered that she could paint recognizable people. One day in January she painted seven large newsprint sheets with people. We hung a one-person show of her cheerful paintings. We hadn't intervened in her painting during these months, except honestly to admire her serious style and the attractive finished products. Whatever Leslie painted, she was sure to paint a lot of. We learned this as we reviewed our notes in the logbook. It influenced our judgments about how many times we asked her to repeat other activities. We knew that if she wanted to persevere, she knew how to.

Amanda began her year with as distinct a style as Leslie's. Her pattern was to paint every color on the same spot. Very early in the year we taught her how to cut with scissors, because her paintings called for that. Later in the year her paintings grew very social, peopled with pretty little girls and decorated with flowers. The monoliths made way for lighter fare, and we followed Amanda's progress by logging it, not interfering in it.

Logging serves the serious, grownup purpose of solving problems with staff direction and priorities. It also makes each of us see more of the fun of the classroom. One day Katherine had been working with Amanda on sewing. After introducing the children to sewing with styrofoam trays we go on to sew with cloth and embroidery hoops, because they give the children a clear field to look at and the cloth doesn't get bunched up. The only tricky part is that the needle has to go back in the cloth on the side where it came out, rather than around the hoop. This problem confused Amanda, who was new at sewing, until suddenly Katherine saw Amanda see the solution to her problem, catch on, and light up! When we sit down to log, it's fun to swap stories about children growing smart.

Leslie was building with blocks one day, when I stopped by and admired her work. She told me she was building an airplane, so I asked if she had ever been in an airplane. She nodded, and I asked where she had gone. She looked at me with great surprise and mild disdain, saying, "Up in the sky!"

When a child is in your care, you must function as if you know who she or he is at any given moment. The danger is that you can delude yourself into thinking that in fact you do have that knowledge. You can reduce this danger by regularly observing and recording behavior, whether or not it fits your preconceptions.

Think about the child who is on your mind. Ask yourself: "What is the worst thing this kid does, the thing that affects my head, heart, soul, peace?" Write down this answer before reading on.

Now study your answer and ask yourself: "What's the name of the feeling I get when this child does this thing?" And work with your feelings, taking responsibility for who you are in this situation. Transactional analysis (see Eric Berne, *Games People Play*) is good for working in this way. Have your adult talk to your child. Deal with your parent and his or her demands on you.

The point of the exercise is that we teachers are in danger of dealing with problems we have with children as if the problem belonged only to the child. If you can find that thing in you which rebels against what the child does, you're on your way home. At our most resourceful we can avoid warfare between the child in us and the children we teach. At Teachers College I studied with Sheila Sullivan who, with some others, was exploring what they called "schoology," in contrast to "education" or "pedagogy." Their concern for "carrying out teaching performance with the greatest possible care" has stayed with me, as has their notion that one devotes substantial teaching energy to "getting the goods" on a child. This posits that a teacher must immediately begin teaching each child, even when there hasn't been time to find out who that child is.

At registration, Kathye couldn't put the ladder blocks together, although we give this toy to children first because it's easy and satisfactory to them. Not only did she not succeed at the ladder blocks, but she wandered off and picked up Lukash's box of slides and spilled them on the floor. I was upset because the pictures were part of our program to make Lukash feel good about himself, and because this little girl was starting school on the wrong foot. Her grandmother watched, while I explained to Kathye, with much severity and emphasis, that she can't just grab stuff at school. Grandmother said she thought we were the kind of school Kathye needed. She told us that Kathye walked at twenty months, and talked at two years. I "got the goods" on this child that she is slow and babyish. By the end of the intake interview we had learned that Kathye, although not yet four, is the eldest of three children, so we had further insight into her need to be a baby. Later we learned that her mother is 19 years old, a child herself although mother of three.

All through the year, Kathye's approach to any new work was that it was too hard for her, that she couldn't do it. She cried often. And yet, little by little, she came to see herself as somebody who could do things well. At the end of the year we were concerned that this pride was still very fragile, and recommended to her mother that she consider letting Kathye repeat prekindergarten. This advice wasn't taken. We can only hope that Kathye found good support as she went on.

Terry was absent a lot at the beginning of school, and we asked her mother if we could help. She needed a sitter after school, it turned out, not just for Terry but also for her little son, Joe. We asked Amanda's mother, thinking that Amanda, an only child, needed a little girl to play with after school. The system they devised has worked beautifully. Amanda, however, showed all the classic signs of sibling jealousy toward Terry and Joe, and needed to know that there's enough love for them all. So we recommended Ann Herbert Scott's wonderful story, *On Mother's Lap*, with beautiful illustrations of Eskimo children, drawn by Glo Coalson. It's a very simple tale of a little boy being rocked on his mother's lap, he hops off to get a toy, then comes back and rocks and rocks; then he gets more toys and rocks and rocks, till the lap gets very full. Then Baby cries, so Mother says "She'd like to rock, too," and the little boy says "There isn't room." But Mother says "Let's see." And sure enough, the baby fits on too. The moral of the story is that there's always enough room on mother's lap. We hope that logging keeps us as wise as the mother in the book; it's our way of trying to balance 20 children on two laps.

5

Visitors and volunteers: Gifts from the community

So, with a nod of thanks to his friends, he went on with his walk through the forest, humming proudly to himself. But, Christopher Robin looked after him lovingly, and said to himself, "Silly old Bear!"

—*Winnie-the-Pooh*

We have many visitors and very few rules for them, except that they must interact with the children. When I visit early childhood programs where visitors are supposed to maintain a low profile, duck their heads when approached by children, and look busy and unresponsive, I think that a great resource is being denied these children.

As a visitor I feel righteous anger when children are denied encounter with me in the name of institutional discipline or "program." If visiting adults are honest in responding to the children and the program, I think they bring richness to any classroom.

Our most frequent visitors are parents, of course. And we believe that parents should always be welcome in their children's classroom. But I also believe that parents need time away from their children. My current view is that, in the community where I've been teaching, most parents' need for time apart outweighs their need to participate at school.

When they do come to participate we ask them what their preference is, to watch and respond to children or to lead activities. We give them the work they choose, and small groups of children to work with, so their experience is satisfactory, not grueling. It's usually a treat for the visitor's child, and sometimes gives school the stamp of approval that a child has been waiting for, making school a real, legitimate place to spend time in.

Most parents are sensitive to the rhythm of the classroom and add to it. Occasionally, when many parents come at once, the room begins to echo with parental-type scolding and fussing. As a parent I realize how scarce patience can become. As a teacher, however, I ask visiting parents to bring a lot of it to their children's school. When parents visit, Katherine and I try to model peaceful ways for parents to deal with children's energy and enthusiasm.

One fall my friend Ronna Jacobs, an accomplished teacher, asked if she could come to school on the first day. I was delighted to say yes, because her sensitive attention to children always enriches the classroom. There were only a couple of times when we really needed her work that day, but it was an extra pleasure to have someone see how nicely things were going, and reflect it back. When we sat down to log, she made us the wonderful offer to return as a regular volunteer. She was in the classroom, as volunteer and substitute, about thirty times through the year.

When Ronna first came, she told me at the logging table that she'd felt nervous watching Lukash climb on the side of the slide. I told her Lukash can handle it, and if he's not interfering with anybody else, nobody will suffer from it. "But since it bothers you, tell Lukash that you don't want him to do it." Ronna modelled talking about feelings when she ended up telling him, "Lukash, I get worried when you climb up high on the slide, so please do your climbing on the monkey bars instead."

A visitor who acts in direct conflict with something I've thought through about my teaching is asked to stop and discuss it with me later.

For example, parents in our community often place very little value on drawing, seeing it as foolish play, not productive work. These same parents are very pleased when their children learn to write letters and numbers. I'm convinced that drawing can open children up to their inner power and is of enormous value. I also teach children to read, and sometimes to write. It seems valuable to encourage the children to relax and draw, so I prohibit writing letters on drawing, except to sign a finished drawing. When an artist friend visited school, she wrote words on her drawing. I think it's fine for her to mix writing and drawing. She was working with Lucretia who has only been praised at home for her writing, never her drawing. I want Lucretia to know she can make wonderful pictures without writing on them. So I asked my artist friend not to model mixing the two.

The teacher who must choose between protecting a child's feelings or an adult's should remember that the classroom is there for the children. The biggest problem with adults in the classroom comes when they forget this, and try to meet their own needs without somehow doing right by the children. It goes against the grain of nice adults to be impatient with children, but sometimes, as with Abby (see Part I, Chapter 3) it's just what children need. If your visitors inhibit you from giving Abby the impatience due her, then your policy on visitors needs to change so Abby comes first.

The Discovery Room for Children was known as a good center and had many offers of help. Some were specialized, like an architect who built us furniture and an attorney who helped us fight City Hall; others were just good people, who liked little children and helped us teach them. Unfortunately, there also came a kind of volunteer who admired the children's beauty and was generous, but rejected the children's need to be taken seriously. I feel I have to ask destructive people to stay away. If an adult can find health by working for children, then that healing is welcome, as long as it's incidental. But when there's a conflict between those needs, the children must be served.

6

Clothing exchange:
Reaching out to parents

Kanga was down below tying the things on, and calling out to Owl, "You won't want this dirty old dish-cloth any more, will you, and what about this carpet, it's all in holes," and Owl was calling back indignantly, "Of course I do! It's just a question of arranging the furniture properly, and it isn't a dish-cloth, it's my shawl."

— *The House at Pooh Corner*

Alliance between home and school comes slowly. For instance, the twins' mother had been bringing them to school erratically. When I phoned she said she was sick. I said that if she lets us know when there's a problem bringing the children to school, we'll try to help out, since we can only teach the children when they're present. We feel that the mother isn't putting enough energy into finding support for her childrearing. Her children don't think well of themselves, and they are poorly informed. We hope to show her that it's okay to need and use other people's help raising her children. She can't do it alone without short-changing them. Nobody can. Many neighbors and others are willing to lend a hand. She may not yet be able to trust someone white and professional like me, but we have greater hopes of her accepting Katherine's lead.

To try to draw this woman and others like her into a larger childrearing community, we developed our clothing exchange. This is how it works. When the sign first goes up some parents explain how they already have systems for passing along outgrown or misbegotten clothing. Others get behind the project, bringing in bags and parcels of clothing daily until The Day. That morning, Katherine and I, along with Esselene Stancil, our wonderful housekeeper, arrange a "shop" putting all the dresses in one place, the baby clothes in another, etc. Our first exchange redistributed 150 garments among 12 families. The second was twice as large. Everyone left with something, and the twins' mother took the odds and ends that remained, saying she'd find homes for them all. Helping her mother carry out that big pile of clothes, Deena called across the room in the most grownup voice I've heard from her yet, "Thank you, Sydney, f'all these nice cloes you givin' us!" With great pleasure in her unaccustomed assertiveness I reminded her that it wasn't me giving, that we were all sharing.

We had to help Hamid's mother feel comfortable about taking clothing. She is Arabic, and taking used or free clothing may be difficult for her people. The Black women helped her find suitable clothing for her three babies, and when she left she seemed quite pleased with her finds.

On Monday Leslie took a quick look at the shop corner, now restored to tape recorder and puzzles, and said to me, "We don't got no cloes here today!"

7

Permission to play:
Field trips

*"We are all going on an Expedition," said Christopher Robin, as he got up and
brushed himself . . . .*

*"Going on an Expotition?" said Pooh eagerly. "I don't think I've ever been on one
of those. Where are we going to on this Expotition?"*

"Expedition, silly old Bear. It's got an 'x' in it."

"Oh," said Pooh. "I know." But he didn't really.

—Winnie-the-Pooh

I like to do field trips and especially enjoy the relationships parents and teachers
develop on them. Nothing else generates quite the same holiday feeling. I don't,
however, build the program around field trips, as do some of my respected
colleagues. Most of the time we stay in the classroom because it shelters our
curriculum. What's in the room helps children express their emotions, and control, test, and master the environment. They are more dependent everywhere
else.

Field trips help children learn about the world outside. Our classroom helps
children learn about the world inside. We emphasize the inner world, though I
respect teachers choosing to have the children learn repeatedly and well about
their environment.

When we do go on a trip we get as many parents as possible to come, and
then divide responsibility for the children. Staff members take the difficult children if their parents don't come, while parents and aunties take two and three of
their own and other well-behaved children. Relaxed and congenial, parents and
teachers tell each other about the children.

We schedule most field trips for spring, when communication between adults
and children is quite clear, instead of making ponderous rule systems to protect
us all in the fall, when children are less likely to pay us any mind.

I prefer the little field trip, like the one to the Junior Museum to handle animals. This one's important because I don't provide animals in our classroom, for
fear I'd communicate my distaste to the children. Before we leave the school, I

urge the parents: "You don't have to like the animals, but please, dislike them silently. Let's let the children experience their own joy in them, without stumbling on our bad trips."

My big moment came when the attendant wrapped herself in a boa constrictor, a seven-foot-long snake, bigger around than a softball, and then asked if any of us would like to wear the snake. Now, I don't like big long snakes as a rule, but when no other adult volunteered, I felt the message the children were getting was alarmist. So I told her I'd wear it if she'd hold its head. It was perfectly clear that the creature was harmless, but the powerful feelings I have about wild creatures tend to cloud my judgment. I turned out to be a successful snake charmer, proud of my courage to teach children better than I had been taught.

Sometimes it's fun to travel in school busses. The children enjoy being in a yellow bus "like big kids," and we can sing and be our own gang on the road. Some children who lack classroom knowhow prove wise on a trip. They may know some city geography, or all the makes of cars. This kind of knowledge enlightens us about children who've decided not to be smart in school. We have a chance to observe them out of our laboratory, to see what attracts them in situations we haven't designed.

Once we went to Golden Gate Park with chicken, charcoal, and starter, to a place with a wonderful playground, where we'd been assured there were fireplaces. We looked at the buffaloes in the paddock and flowers and carp in the conservatory, then unpacked everything, and the children dispersed onto the play equipment. We looked around. There were no fireplaces at all. Is anything so raw as plucked chicken?

The school bus driver sweetly took me to a hardware store where I bought an overpriced hibachi. Back in the park I tried and tried to get a fire started. Half an hour later the parents took over, put the stove behind a wind screen, and started the fire; we ended up with delicious chicken. The parents were indulgent about my failure as a barbecue chef. One father kept telling me that if I'd told him what I had in mind, he'd have gotten the whole thing together for us.

The children love to ride on BART, our subway, to anywhere at all. There's a station we can reach from Burnett by bus. Once you're on BART, if you don't exit you can ride as long as you like for a nominal fee. The children talk about what they see, and I introduce vocabulary: "station," "platform," "track," "train," "underground." The children are delighted when BART emerges from underground, onto an elevated track near our station.

Field trips are best when we adults give ourselves permission to play. I'm not sure what causes that to happen, but it's wonderful when it does.

Not all experiences benefit from immediate demystification: here is the intervention problem in a new light. Sybil Marshall (see Bibliography I) read this poem at a workshop:

CHILD MIND

Eyes open wide
In wonderment
The children pressed against
The classroom window.
I told them to sit down.

John said,
"But Miss! a star has fallen in our field."
I saw no star
'Til, bending down to child height,
There in the grass
I glimpsed the dazzling light.

A star?
A piece of broken jam-jar
Catching the rays of a low January sun.
Educationally, it would have been sound
To follow up with a lesson
On refraction
And the properties of glass.

I couldn't
To forty children
Who had just seen a star.

—Author unknown

A classic problem arises when children come to dislike field trips because they are always made to reinterpret them back at school. Assignments we all hated didn't speak to our new perceptions, but were proofs to the teacher that we had paid attention to whatever the trip was supposed to teach us.

Striking a balance is hard. I do find it interesting, every once in a while, to assign work to some children the day after the field trip. The day after we saw bison at Golden Gate Park, a kid named Andre made the best buffalo picture I've ever seen—it had five legs and was rather skinny, but it buffaloed.

So, while it's not always useful to recreate the trip the following day in song and story, when the children do have some new constructs to express, we let them. If there's a buffalo picture inside a child's head, we're on course when we ask the child to draw it. It's hard to know what's in somebody's head, though, so the safest policy is to provide the paint and see what happens. When we're standing on a BART elevated platform and Emily asks, "Can you stand here and look 'til morning?" the pure poetry warms us.

8

Graduation:
The mountain top

Piglet said nothing, but just stood and glowed.
Never before had anyone sung ho for Piglet (PIGLET) ho all by himself. When
it was over, he wanted to ask for one of the verses over again, but didn't quite like to. It
was the verse beginning "O gallant Piglet," and it seemed to him a very thoughtful
way of beginning a piece of poetry.

—The House at Pooh Corner

Our graduation reminds the parents that their children are smart, that they should stand up for such terrific children and clear the way for them to continue to learn so well. It also tells the children that they're good at school and that they should be proud, because they've done good work and learned a lot and grown. Graduation should be a recital of things that the grownups know the children learned at school.

Several weeks before graduation I like to take care of the practical details of promoting children to new environments. A meeting is held to inform parents of their options and their power, and to show them how to continue the reading program on their own, after school is over.

This is how the meeting went one year:

First a survey was made to find a convenient time.

Two notices went out, one a week before the meeting, one the day before, including an amendable agenda.

The meeting was held at dismissal time. Childcare was provided for the graduating children and their siblings by our psychologist and social worker. If parents who came for their children had forgotten the meeting, they were encouraged to attend anyway.

I introduced and greeted the 15 parents, grandparents, and babysitters of our 16 children.

Katherine invited additions to the agenda, and wrote them on the chalkboard. The final agenda:

What you can do about picking a kindergarten for your child.
How children are assigned to classes.
What options parents have.
How to choose a kindergarten.
How to visit a school effectively.
What to look for.
Reports from parents who already have children in nearby schools.

How can you keep up and extend the reading the children have learned this year?
Why what you do is important.
Demonstrations (with children) of techniques, games.
Discussion.
Sharing other ideas; conclusions.

The parents exchange enormous gifts of power and support for the problems they face in educating their children despite the racist, hostile system. As they inform each other of options and their pitfalls, Katherine and I begin to let go of our stewardship over their children. This letting go continues through the graduation, and if we are thoughtful, the ceremony completes it.

The day before graduation the children take home a book of work: stories they've dictated, pictures they've drawn and painted, photographs and slides we've taken of them, their reading words and some blank reading cards and a marker for the family to add new vocabulary. We don't want the importance of the book to get lost in the ceremony and feasting, so we give it its own day.

Parents make a party of the graduation, creating a general air of excitement by dressing up their children, by bringing their whole family including aunts, grandfathers, cousins, nephews and close friends, by bringing food to share and cameras.

Our graduation one year:

1. Three songs sung by the children.
2. The logic exercise, done once in turn by each child in response to my holding up a pair of objects: "They're both markers but they're not the same color, this one is yellow and this one is green."
3. The assertiveness exercise in which I tell Leslie she's an elephant and she says "No, you're wrong," and then I tell Buck he's at school and he says "Yes, you're right." Each child in turn judges one statement and affirms or denies it.
4. Reading. Three sentences per child, including:
   John eats chicken.
   Batman loves milk.

I love 2-wheeler.
Good hot sauce.
Deena loves swing.
Buck can choke monster.
Junior can ride 2-wheeler.

5. Poetry. Each child recited either "One, Two, Buckle my Shoe" or
   Sometimes, when I skip or hop
   Or even when I'm jumping
   Suddenly, I like to stop
   And listen to me, thumping.

6. A final spectacular song, *My Pigeon House,* which the children learned by listening many times to a tape recording, and sang with elaborate gestures.

7. Katherine then read them their diplomas one by one. Each diploma was different, and they went like this:
   "We are very proud of Amanda. She can read 38 words and count to 39. She has become very strong on the climbing bars and stopped being so bossy. She can ride the 2-wheeler and do every puzzle in the school."

8. Katherine presented each graduate with a box of watercolors from the school's supply for a gift.

9. I made a one-minute speech about the importance of keeping the schools aware that your children have adults behind them, people who care what happens to them.

10. Then we paraded back from the auditorium to our room for a gala pot-luck dinner.

The graduation celebrates the intervention of the school in the children's education. How sad it would be if they had not shown progress. Left alone, people grow. Schools must be held accountable to see that their every intervention cultivates and nurtures children's lives.

Perspective
Empowering parents

Here is Edward Bear, coming downstairs now, bump, bump, bump, on the back of his head, behind Christopher Robin. It is, as far as he knows, the only way of coming downstairs, but sometimes he feels that there really is another way, if only he could stop bumping for a moment and think of it.

—Winnie-the-Pooh

While still an undergraduate at the University of Chicago, I decided not to pit myself against parents of the children I teach. I had a summer job as counselor of seven-year-old girls at the Hyde Park Neighborhood Club. The question of hitting came up, and I said, optimistically, that we weren't going to have any hitting in the group. One youngster said, "But my Mama told me, somebody hits me, I gotta hit 'em back!" I found myself saying to her, "Your Mama's absolutely right, and when you're on the street and somebody hits you, you better hit 'em back. But when you're here with me, I'm supposed to take care of you, and the best way I can take care of kids is if we don't have any hitting. If somebody around here starts hitting you, holler for me so I can take care of you."

As I teach longer, that speech gets shorter. Now I say, "Did your Mama tell you to mind the teacher? Well, I'm the teacher, and in *this* school we don't have any hitting because we want it safe here."

Ten years later, all the teachers in our "Experienced Teacher Fellowship Program" at Columbia agreed that involving parents in early childhood education was very important. We disagreed only as to whether parents should have 49 or 51 per cent of the power. Because of the strike raging around us that fall of 1968, the question came up again and again.

I was unsure at first. My mind kept running to parent decisions I knew had had bad results for children. There, before us, was the decision of the Ocean Hill-Brownsville parents to adopt the Bereiter-Englemann program in schools which they (temporarily) controlled. I was so opposed to that program that I had reviewed it in the AFT newspaper just about that time, as follows:

The slick packaging of this book makes it doubly dangerous, because the philosophy of education it contains is destructive to children. The program in *Teaching Disadvantaged Children in the Preschool* does not include attempts to free children from anxiety so that they can learn.

It places no importance on materials that teach. It is a rote method.

This book is a pseudo-scholarly, explicit blueprint for a conformity aiming to cram information into children so they can compete successfully in the first grade . . . .

There is no place in their program for games, child-child interaction, 'messy' play, or physical movement. They marshal children through arid group response drills in a highly skilled manner. They provide for neither laughter nor discovery in their program. They reward with cookies and punish with slaps or a dark, isolated room.

They have not learned from Sylvia Ashton-Warner, John Holt, Herb Kohl or direct observation of children at work. They run a school on the authoritarian lines of the early 19th century. I cannot help but believe that they think Black children are still in that century.

So, though theoretically eager to support the goal of parents having 51 per cent of the power, I held back because the Ocean Hill-Brownsville experience showed that concerned parents could be misled by slick packaging of outdated rhetoric. My best professional opinion was that the Ocean Hill-Brownsville decision might better have been left to the professionals. This view was soon shaken out of me.

One colleague in the graduate program, Pearl Draine, had been instrumental in organizing the Child Development Group of Mississippi, which evolved later into Mississippi Head Start. Pearl is Black, an accomplished teacher, and a fighter. She said to me, "Okay, Sydney, let's get down to it. Suppose you were a teacher in Ocean Hill-Brownsville, and the parents said to you, 'We want you to use Bereiter-Englemann.' What would you do?" And I said, "I'd fight with them." Pearl said, "How much would you fight?" I said, "I'd fight until I won." "That's what I mean by community control," she replied. "You have to convince the parents, or you have to follow their lead. But you do get to fight, Sydney. It's a lot of work to fight and win, but then the people you're working for understand what you're about, and that agreement between parents and teachers is real education, real support for children. Once you've put your best arguments to the parents, they own them too, and can use them to make education better everywhere. *The way a good teacher works under parent control is that she teaches the parents all she knows.*"

I was convinced by that argument. I adopted Pearl's position that a teacher-parent alliance is best for children. I now choose to trust parents to make good decisions, particularly if we teachers share our concerns and experience with them. Further, the state of the public schools in our inner cities then and now convinces me that even if parents make bad choices, they won't do any worse than our superintendents and school boards.

The Discovery Room, begun a year later, was organized on this principle. One parent from each family was on the Board of Directors of the school, with power to hire and fire staff and with input to the curriculum. A test of our philosophy came very soon. Laura was a director, and her son Jimmy came in one morning saying his mother didn't want him to knit any more. That evening I phoned Laura and we talked for two or three hours, about her fears that knitting would lead to homosexuality, about sex roles and exploration, and about Jimmy as a special, individual boy important to both of us. As the discussion came to an end I told Laura that we would only give Jimmy knitting if he came and told us she'd changed her mind. I hung up my phone hoping Pearl was right, for a lot was at stake beyond Jimmy's knitting. I felt the whole future of the school hung in the balance.

The next morning Jimmy told me he had his mother's permission to knit. And he did, until he discovered some wood and took up sawing, like the fickle, delightful child he was.

Discovery Room parents didn't bother with most of the school's decisions. They certainly didn't want to be involved in deciding how much toilet paper or what kinds of toys to buy. But they were astute about hiring and firing. We had a parent who worked part-time at the school. She seemed unwilling to learn to use positive reinforcement of children's behavior. She was black, and had I had to fire her singlehandedly, as a white center director I'd have been vulnerable. Instead, I asked the personnel committee to decide the issue. I knew I wanted her out, but firing her would only work if it were clearly on educational and not racist grounds. They heard both sides and fired the woman. She left without rancor, even keeping her son in the program.

Our Discovery Room, like other community-controlled schools of that period, was trying to be relevant to poor people as well as to a responsible concept of early education. Our schools were places for children to flower. We trained teachers to expect commitment from parents, and parents to expect teachers to be caring and competent. The center functioned well because the roles of parents and staff were differentiated: parents made policy and staff kept parents informed about our work with their children. We teachers had to enlighten and share our competence. We would win or lose each disputed point based on how well we made our case.

Working for parents, the staff tend to discuss ideas and seek consensus before bringing them to the Board. Working alongside others who also believe that the clients should have control over their children's care and education means that each individual on staff has a forum in which to develop his or her priorities. (Paul Goodman discusses this problem at length in his book, *Drawing the Line*.)

If the parents don't accept something central to one's philosophy, and one isn't willing to give it up, then one must find other parents to work for.

It is especially important for a staff to discuss policy among themselves when there is a wide cultural mix in the school. I always try to consult Black colleagues and friends when making ethically difficult decisions about Black children.

Working for the San Francisco Unified School District, where there's no provision for a parent board, I try to behave as if there were one. Decisions that I would take to a board, if I were working for one, I take to the parents at the prekindergarten.

Because they have no official power, the parents at Burnett are often uninterested in setting priorities. They tell me to use my best judgment. That too is a choice. But when the AFT called a strike in 1974, I polled the parents: if there's a strike do you want me on the picket line or in the classroom? All said they wanted me teaching, even a parent who worked for the school district as a housekeeper and crossed her own picket line each morning to bring her child to us. (The strike ended with a 7-1/4 per cent raise, despite a Board offer of 7-1/2 per cent prior to the strike.)

How involved should a teacher be with parents? Should we fight the establishment on behalf of children? During the 1968 strike by the United Federation of Teachers against community control of the New York schools, I went with many of my friends, colleagues, and neighbors to reopen schools in the face of the strike. Why? The answer is in a letter I wrote, published in The New York Times on the first day of that strike:

> To the Editor:
>
> I have just resigned my membership in the United Federation of Teachers because of its stand against community control of schools. Raised in the traditions of trade unionism, I find myself deeply grieved to be forced to take this action.
>
> If the parents of the children in my class should ever feel that I was doing their children harm, they should have the right to fire me. It is not the proper function of the union to protect its incompetents against dismissal. In my four years in ghetto schools I have seen highly destructive teachers. I have also found sensitive people in the community who knew which teachers cared about their children.
>
> It seems to me that when Black survival and self-determination are pitted against the job security of a group of teachers—many of whom are inadequate and some vicious—then concerned people must support the Black community and its children.

The UFT won the strike, ensuring that policies would be made by administrators, not parents. The local school boards, with their hope that the schools could liberate the children of the poor from poverty, if their parents could determine school policies and priorities, lost.

Public schools in today's inner cities just don't work. California Governor George Deukmejian made political hay by publicly questioning the propriety of sending children into buildings where their safety is in serious question. Schools have begun requiring releases from parents regarding children's safety during recess and lunch. Junior high and high school children don't go to the bathroom, or go in groups of two and three.

Public schools don't keep their best teachers. Pressured working conditions, ethical vacuums and the seniority system all conspire to send good teachers away.

The communities of America have lost heart about the possibilities of good public education. More and more they refuse to tax themselves so their children can be exploited by bigger bureaucracies and better paid administrators.

The children know the schools don't work, and they are absent in droves. A rate of 30% absenteeism is not uncommon in inner city schools. The way it is now, the Board of Education and the Superintendent's office run the schools as they see fit, the unions represent at least the senior teachers, but no one represents parents and children. We need to change all this, to the point where parents hire and fire administrators and teachers and set priorities, and children, thus protected, are set free to learn.

The rest of this chapter is about school control. I believe, based on the kind of experiences I've had working in New York and San Francisco, or should I say Harlem and Hunters Point schools, that we need to start taking the schools back from the school boards so our children can have the education they deserve. For background and alternatives, I refer you to the Appendix, a perspective on school control by L. Harmon Zeigler and others. Zeigler suggests that public education must now move in one of three directions.

All my experience tells me that his first option—control by the superintendent and professionals—would bring us more attempts to mold children to fit adult convenience.

Option 2—control by the local neighborhood through a decentralized, malleable structure—and option 3—control by parents through some system of vouchers, offer a chance to growing children, since in each of these options the parents have the authority to advocate on their behalf.

In America you get the education you pay for. People who don't hold economic power have to pay for their children's education with their time and enormous amounts of energy. If parents don't show schools their concern and their muscle, children are educated by default. In urban America the best advocates for children are probably their parents. Caring teachers are also good advocates, sometimes from a more informed perspective. But teachers, unlike parents, can walk away from children. Ideally, parents and teachers share information and work jointly on behalf of the children.

State and federal funding for child development programs has for twenty years required some sort of parent input, variously called "parent participation," "parent involvement," or "parent advisory committees." My experience with these is that when people have real power they spend the time and energy necessary to exercise it. However, when they are powerless, wanted merely to rubber stamp someone else's plans, they save their energy. In some Head Starts parents are active and learn advocacy skills. The generally low attendance at parent meetings in public schools reflects the unwillingness of parents to participate in a sham process, though they would be glad to put effort into a real exercise of power.

The interests and problems of the urban middle-class teacher differ from those of the inner-city parent with a child in public school. The teacher may be caught in a web of some or all of the following:

- poor training or training to teach only middle-class suburban children
- rigid yet indifferent employer expectations
- spotty provision for children's medical, dental, psychological and social service needs
- hostility between the community and the school
- irresponsible colleagues, teachers who do not teach
- supervisors who are afraid or inadequate to evaluate teachers
- unions that protect destructive and inept supervisors and teachers from being fired
- Boards of Education concerned with political appearances rather than responsibility to children, and
- a general feeling of inability to control one's own life.

A different web may catch the parent:

- not enough shoes and too many rats
- schools that train children to be soldiers and clerks
- social services that intrude on privacy
- health services that provide supervised neglect
- absence of trees, open space, art, human scale, and graceful surroundings
- the parent's own discomfort with a school system that probably oppressed her/him in childhood
- ambivalence toward books and formal education, and
- a general feeling of inability to control one's own life.

Coming from such different experiences, parents and teachers can't gracefully and swiftly form an alliance on behalf of a child. Nevertheless, one of them must take the initiative to cut through this tangle, inviting the other with clean opening gestures to enter into such an alliance.

When a parent places a high value on schooling, so does her or his child. When a teacher is clearly disposed to form an alliance with the parent, home support of the program becomes more likely.

Power—to hire and fire personnel and to be heard with regard to curriculum—belongs in the hands of those persons most continuously sensitive to children's potential. School boards, teachers, and administrators ought to be sensitive to the needs and desires of parents and children, in order to promote creative education. With parent control, school personnel must respond.

People who oppose local control of schools are afraid that the most repressive, backward, far-rightist kinds of people will get hold of the schools and ruin them. I think they already have. These critics foresee the end to fair hiring procedures, a return to favoritism, and an end to integration. In our public schools today I see the young and the dark being laid off, competence counting for nothing, and neither integration nor local control existing in the inner cities. These same people see the public schools as the great opportunity for poor kids to latch onto the American Dream, and the mixture of middle-class with poor, white with non-white, children from educated families with those from illiterate homes as a solution to important problems in our society. I wish I could agree.

I see that the public schools in the cities are already run by the right and are highly segregated. Parents with other options do not send their children to city schools. I see the schools turning children away from learning and away from children of other colors. I see hiring based solely on paper qualifications, and no attention at all to giftedness in teachers. I see excellent teachers terminated on grounds of seniority alone, while teachers with no gifts at all are retained because they have taught longer in that system.

M. S. Stearns proposes a possible relationship between parents' exercising power in school decision-making and the achievement levels of students:

Model For Parent Involvement

Community Understanding	Program Adaptation	Control of Parent Fate

Parents make recommendations as to how to improve program for their children.

Parents learn of the problems involved in making changes. They learn of constraints on professionals and other reasons for decisions. They become sympathetic and support program.

School program is changed to parents' recommendation; becomes more appropriate to particular children served.

Parents note their effect on shaping school program—feel some control over own environment; communicate this attitude to own children.

Parents communicate importance of program to other parents and own children.

CHILDREN'S LEVEL OF ACHIEVEMENT RISES

(Adapted from "Parental Involvement in Compensatory Education Programs," see Bibliography I.)

What is missing from inner city public schools are support systems: for children, so they can learn without guilt, failure, and humiliation, and for teachers, so they can talk about what works and what doesn't, spreading the former and solving the latter without fear of being exposed and vulnerable.

In hopes of building such protection and support we must seek out and encourage any constitutional alternative which takes the control of children's education away from politically motivated, distant school boards and faceless administrative staffs, and returns it to parents, neighbors, and small agencies which can serve to protect children in those few cases where their parents can't. It won't be easy for parents to reclaim responsibility for education, but it must happen.

Appendix

The following article by L. Harmon Zeigler, Harvey J. Tucker, and L.A. Wilson II appeared in *Intellect* magazine, September, 1976. It provides a background for discussing control of schools. The authors are all from the Center for Educational Policy and Management, University of Oregon, at Eugene.

School boards and community power: The irony of professionalism

According to reports of the most recent outbreaks of violence in Boston and Louisville, parental objections to busing are generated by a perceived "loss of control" over education. It is the thesis of this article that the process whereby parents lost control of education began well before the current dispute over busing. It may be true that the sense of helplessness first became obvious when the buses began to roll. However, it is helpful to view the process of parental political disenfranchisement as one which has occurred in phases. Accordingly, we offer the following timetable of what has transpired in American education: Phase I, the period of "maximum feasible participation" (1835-1900); Phase II, the period of "reform" and "efficiency" (1900-54); Phase III, the period in which the school became viewed as an agent of social and economic change (1954-75); and Phase IV, (1975-), during which the aspirations of Phase III will be proved unachievable, albeit laudable. The loss of control over education began in Phase II, when schools began to professionalize. Today, school districts constitute one-fifth of the 78,000 units of local government. The dilemma of diminished impact of citizens on these structures captures the tension of the growing struggle in society between the contradicting demands of experts and laymen. Similar struggles are becoming increasingly characteristic of governmental systems grown too large and complex to be managed efficiently unless lay participation is minimized.

Phase I: Lay Control (1835-1900)

During Phase I, control of American education rested with local boards of education. There was substantial opportunity for laymen to influence members of their boards. At that time, there were more school boards (as late as 1930, there were approximately 130,000 independent school districts; now there are about 15,000 school districts), and, since each school district had a school board—and frequently neighborhood boards—the opportunity for participation was substantial. As school systems increased in size, lay boards found that they could not effectively attend to the day-to-day operation of schools. They reasoned that they were quite capable of performing routine tasks, but simply lacked the time. Thus, they commonly appointed a "superintendent." However, the superintendent's responsibilities were usually strictly clerical, and did not involve participation in policy decisions such as staffing and curriculum. Clearly, the norm of active lay administration was powerful. To those familiar with the 1960's argument for "community control," such a system may seem ideal. A lay board, responsible to a small constituency, governed education. Who could object?

Reformers objected, and the reform movement in urban politics (Phase II) marked the beginning of the decline of lay control. The reformers' objections to community control were not without substance. The ward-based electoral system for school boards shared all the advantages and disadvantages of the urban political machines of the era. Urban machines, in performing the function of integrating immigrants into political life, rewarded votes with jobs. Since, in most cases, local school districts were coterminous with municipal wards, there was a substantial amount of patronage in the awarding of teaching and administrative positions. The currency of political machines was patronage, and education was no exception. On the positive side, political machines were acutely sensitive to the potential alienation of the various ethnic minorities which formed the majority coalition. In New York, Boss Tweed's ward board of education, for example, allowed the various native tongues to be taught and removed textbooks which contained alleged slurs about immigrant groups. Indeed, Tweed's school system may sound like the promised land to modern critics who decry the loss of cultural identity among minority groups.

Political machines were—as the reformers charged—"corrupt." They siphoned off funds from building contracts, awarded contracts on the basis of political influence, rather than competitive bidding, and allowed bribery by textbook salesmen. Teachers had to pay machine functionaries for positions and academic qualifications played a minor role. Thus, school politics, like the machine politics of the urban area of which they were a part, provided responsiveness and corruption. Nevertheless, school policy-making reflected the values of the subgroups within the community. In working-class areas, working-class values prevailed. In upper class areas, upper class values prevailed. In any case, "the people," for better or worse, were not excluded from the making of educational policy.

Phase II: Control by Local Professionals (1900-54)

The reform movement can be accurately described as one of a largely Protestant elite's response to lay control. The reform movement, by fostering major structural changes in the governing structure of education, was consciously designed to reduce lay responsibility for education. It was a class-based movement aimed at shifting the control of schools from laymen to experts.

The reform movement's major structural modifications were the centralization of school administration, to be accomplished both by the destruction of the authority of community boards and by the merger of small districts into larger ones; the abolition of ward-based elections; the election of board members by non-partisan ballots; and the separation of board elections from other municipal and state elections. The philosophy behind these structural changes was to substitute "scientific management" for political influence.

A necessary corollary for structural change was an expansion of the role of the superintendent, to be achieved at the expense of the board. Reliance on "experts," then, played as large a role in the reform movement as did structural modification to reduce the influence of political machines. If the political machines, with their strong immigrant base, were designed to give power to *the* people, the upper-class response was to provide power to *their* people—the experts. Some reformers couched their biases against the lower classes in phrases such as efficiency, while others were quite open in their assertion that only "successful" people should serve on school boards. Such people, from businesses and professions, could be expected to defer to the superintendent.

The shift in the composition of boards of education was dramatic. Not only did they become fewer and smaller, but they also lost the representative character typical of Phase I. In St. Louis, reformers were successful in persuading the Missouri legislature to approve a new charter requiring the non-partisan at-large election of school board members. The purpose of this new charter—the keynote of the reform movement—was to take the schools out of "politics" to eliminate the machine. The charter was approved in 1897. In 1896, professionals and businessmen constituted 14% of the board; in 1897, they constituted 83%. By 1927, the year of the first systematic national survey of the origins of board members, the St. Louis pattern was typical. Reformers had succeeded in eliminating the working class by exchanging the previous politics of patronage for the "apolitical" politics of upper-class "public-regarding" behavior. Boards were composed of white, Anglo-Saxon Protestants, who were wealthy and well-educated, but not representative. The reforms had clearly done their work well.

Local boards of education were not only reflective of the social class of the reformers. Their willingness to yield authority to the superintendent—a consequence of the business orientation of the upper classes—was congruent with the tenets of sound management so clearly a part of the reform ideology. Superintendents evolved from clerks to policy-makers because boards wanted them to do so.

As the reform movement achieved its goals, colleges of education began the production and distribution of experts in educational administration. By 1913, schools of education had become cohesive in their philosophy and well-connected with urban reformers. A handful of influential educators took the lead in developing an ideology of administration, instilling the ideology in future superintendents, and placing them in key superintendencies.

By the 1960's, the average superintendent's professional staff numbered 150. This professional staff administers the most costly governmental activity in most communities, and the position of the superintendent is, in comparison to his local counterparts, visible and prestigious. Superintendents are more widely known among the general public than the local Congressman, and their salaries are normally higher than city managers. In contrast, public awareness of school board activity is slight. Most people cannot name anything their school board has done in the last year; most do not identify the board as being responsible for public representation within the school system; and a substantial minority do not think school boards have legal authority over school administrators.

In fact, most board members do not view their role as representing, or speaking for, "the public." Rather, they view their role as speaking *for* the administration *to* the "public." Such views are a natural consequence of reform. Lacking a constituency (as a consequence of at-large elections), and lacking a systematc recruitment mechanism (as a consequence of nonpartisanship), they are normally recruited through the civic-business elite, sometimes by the existing board. Boards view their service as one of the civic responsibilities of the guardian class. Since, in most cases, boards have no independent staff, the agenda for meetings is set by the administration. Setting the agenda is a highly significant political function, as it defines what is to be decided. It is not surprising, therefore, that school boards solicit and defer to policy recommendations from superintendents. School boards typically enact policies suggested by their professional staff in about 85% of the recorded votes. Such a percentage of success would be the envy of any president, governor, or mayor.

The bureaucratic system worked quite well as long as the goals of education were narrowly defined. The basic problem to be solved by educational planners was how to homogenize an immigrant population, to infuse it with a consistent set of values, and to reduce conflict—in short, to manufacture a cohesive society. In this situation, it was reasonable to centralize administration.

However, in the last stages of Phase II, new demands (and revivals of old demands) were placed on schools. From the Federal government came the demand (beginning with Brown v. Board of Education) that schools serve as agents of social change. From minority populations came demands for "community control" —an inadvertent plea for a return to Phase I.

Phase III: The Nationalization of Education (1954-75)

As Phase II drew to a close, two irreconcilable sets of demands were being placed upon schools—that they serve as agents of social change and that they be returned to the people. To meet the latter was to deny the former, since the major thrust for social change has never originated locally.

Phase III, then, is characterized by an erosion of the authority of the local administration by the imposition of Federal mandates. The consequence of Phase II was a loss of lay control to the local superintendent. In Phase III, the superintendents lost control to Federal agencies.

The intervention of the Federal government in education has had a consistent pattern, whether the source of the intervention is the courts, the Congress, or the Department of Health, Education, and Welfare. The national government has intervened to increase the educational and, by inference, economic opportunities of deprived populations. In becoming the spokesman for the underprivileged, the national government was responding to demands which local schools could not meet. Being deliberately designed as non-responsive and insulated, the latter had little communication with spokesmen of undereducated populations. As curators of the status quo, schools had a vested interest in preferential education.

The Brown ruling shifted the arena of decision from local to national government. Henceforth, school administration would devote an increasing amount of energy to legal defense before Federal courts, losing with each adverse decision the power accumulated during Phase II. Local authority was further constrained by the establishment of desegregation guidelines in 1965 and 1966 by the Department of Health, Education, and Welfare. Legal action initiated by HEW and the Justice Department established a highly visible base of Federal influence. The Federal bureaucracy involved itself still further with the passage of the Elementary and Secondary Education Act of 1965 (ESEA), which doubled the Federal contribution to educational funding and placed a strong monetary emphasis upon its concern with equality of educational opportunity.

In its implementation, ESEA created a new pattern of bureaucratic interaction. Local schools, to compete for Federal grants, hired administrators to write grant proposals. When proposals were funded, more administrators were recruited to maintain the programs. Thus, the local bureaucracy expanded to do business with a national bureaucracy. In some urban districts, the size of the administrative staff tripled between 1966 and 1975, while the number of students and staff remained constant. Relationships between the new sets of local and HEW bureaucrats were generally cordial and the influx of Federal funds was welcome. The gradual nationalization of school policy was based on the assumption that local school districts lacked the resources or inclination to implement the changes necessary for racial and economic equality in the schools.

The Coleman Report revealed, however, that differences in school facilities and curriculum were not related to the achievement of students. Logically, therefore, increased expenditures, and the various innovations of ESEA, were pointless. The most important single factor affecting achievement was family background and the family background of fellow students. Further analysis revealed that black children attending predominantly black schools had lower achievement scores and lower aspirations than black students with comparable family backgrounds who attended white schools. The policy implications were clear. The only way to improve the educational and, hence, economic opportunities of blacks was to forcibly assign them to middle-class or white schools, and to assign middle-class whites to black schools, or both.

Although executive and legislative support for busing ranged from neutral to obstructionist, the legal argument was sound—court-ordered busing began, and, with it, the attendant violence and protests. Protesting to the superintendent was pointless, so parents first tried to influence the Federal bureaucracy and courts, then, finally, emulated the blacks of the 1960's and took to the streets. Their rhetoric was contained, essentially, in one demand: give us back our schools. However, as we have seen, this demand was three-quarters of a century too late.

Education and Social Goals

The evidence gradually accumulating strongly implies that the use of schools as agents of social change—specifically for the equalization of economic opportunity—cannot be successful. In 1972, Jencks' analysis concluded that school reform "cannot bring about significant social changes . . . ." Jencks addressed himself explicitly to the goal of equal economic opportunity. Another investigator, Boudon, echoed Jencks' conclusions, arguing that society, rather than schools, is responsible for inequality of economic opportunity. Boudon offered the astonishing conclusion that "educational growth as such has the effect of increasing rather than decreasing social and economic inequality, even in the case of an educational system that becomes more equalitarian."

If these researchers are right, Phase III is misguided. If schools can not serve as agents of social change, the philosophical underpinnings of Federal intervention are flawed. What, then, for the future?

The first issue which must be solved is the status of the social goal of economic equality. If we retain the social goal, there are two options. We can accept the judgment that schools, as now constituted, cannot reduce inequality of economic opportunity, but also assume that they could if they were allowed to expand their sphere of control over the child. Specifically, schools would have to combat the disabling effects of class and family by assuming more control over the child at an earlier age. Formal schooling would have to begin as soon as cognitively feasible, and the role of the family would have to be minimized. School administration would, of necessity, be conducted at the national level by educational professionals.

As an alternative, we can accept the judgment that schools cannot reduce inequality of economic opportunity and abandon them as a means to this end. The goal could be achieved by several other means. We could establish political controls over economic institutions—a process normally referred to as socialism. Alternatively, we could simply reduce actual inequality by legislative fiat. For instance, Congress could legislate that no individual can receive less than $10,000 or more than $50,000 in annual income, and institute a system of reverse taxation to achieve this goal, bypassing the process of education entirely.

If we retain the social goal and insist on achieving it through the schools, the consequence for school governance is increased centralization of decision locus and expansion of authority. If, however, we either abandon the social goal or abandon schools as the means of achieving it, several options for school governance are possible.

1. We can retain the primacy of professional educational standards, while increasing the importance of local concerns by returning to Phase II. We can return the superintendent and local educational professionals to their former positions of influence, and accept minimal parental control of the educational process.

2. We can regard schooling as an end in itself, and seek to make it as pleasant as possible for the student and parents. One way this can be achieved is by undoing the work of the reformers—i.e., halt centralization and professionalization and return the schools to the conditions that existed prior to 1900. The result would be "community control."

3. Another, more extreme, option is to assume that, while education is a public good, and hence subject to public finance, the content and process of education are private matters. Thus, a system of vouchers could be instituted. Every parent could be given a governmental education voucher to be used for the child's education in any school, freely chosen by parents. Schools which could not successfully compete for vouchers would be closed. Private choice would thus be substituted for public choice. The result would be "individual control."

American education is in an untenable position because Phase III governance can not achieve its mandate. Whether the goal of economic equality is retained or abandoned, a change in the pattern of control over education seems inevitable. The options range from extreme centralization to maximum individual control. However, in no case should the choice be clouded by unrealistic expectations about what formal education can accomplish.

Bibliography I

Books for child-centered teachers

Adams, C. and Fay, J. *No More Secrets: Protecting Your Child From Sexual Assault*, Impact Publishers, P.O. Box 1094, San Luis Obispo, CA 93406, 1981

Arbuthnot, M.H. *The Arbuthnot Anthology of Children's Literature*, N.Y. Lothrop, Lee & Shepard, 1976

Ashton-Warner, S. *Spinster*, N.Y. Simon and Schuster, 1963

Ashton-Warner, S. *Teacher*, N.Y. Bantam, 1964

Baumrind, D. "Socialization and Instrumental Competence in Young Children," in *Young Children*, Vol. XXVI, No. 2, December, 1970. Washington, D.C., National Association for the Education of Young Children.

Berne, E. *Games People Play*, N. Y. Grove Press, 1964

Cohen, D. *Observing and Recording the Behavior of Young Children*, N.Y. Teachers College Press, Columbia, 1958

Coons, J. and Sugarman, S. *Education by Choice*, Berkeley, University of California Press, 1978

Dennison, G. *The Lives of Children*, N.Y. Random House, 1969

Dreikurs, R. *Children, the Challenge*, N.Y. Hawthorn, 1964

Goodman, P. *Drawing the Line*, N.Y. Random House, 1962

Goodman, P. *The Empire City*, N.Y. Bobbs Merrill, 1959

Gordon, S. *Let's Make Sex a Household Word*, N.Y. John Day, 1975

Hartley, R. *Complete Book of Children's Play*, N.Y. Apollo, 1970

Hearne, B. *Choosing Books for Children*, N.Y. Dell, 1982

Hendricks, G. and Wills, R. *The Centering Book*, N.Y. Prentice-Hall (Spectrum), 1975

Holt, J. *How Children Fail*, N.Y. Pitman, 1967

Huber, M.B. *Story and Verse for Children*, N.Y. Macmillan, 1940

Hunt, J. McV. *Intelligence and Experience*, N.Y. Ronald, 1961

Isaacs, S. *Intellectual Growth in Young Children*, N.Y. Schocken, 1966

Isaacs, S. *Social Development in Young Children*, N.Y. Schocken, 1966

Kozol, J. *Free Schools*, Boston, Houghton Mifflin, 1972

Levin, H.M., ed. *Community Control of Schools*, N.Y. Simon and Schuster (Clarion), 1970

Marshall, S. *An Experiment in Education*, Cambridge (England) Cambridge University Press, 1968

Montessori, M. *The Montessori Method*, Cambridge MA, R. Bentley, 1964

Moustakas, C. *The Authentic Teacher*, Cambridge MA, Doyle, 1967

Murphy, G. *Freeing Intelligence Through Teaching*, N.Y. Harper, 1961

Nuffield Math Project, *Pictorial Representation*, N.Y. John Wiley, 1969

Paley, V. *White Teacher*, Cambridge, MA, Harvard University Press

Pavenstedt, E. *The Drifters*, Boston, Little, Brown, 1967

Rockwell, R. *Hug a Tree*, Mt. Rainier MD, Gryphon House, 1983

Schrag, P. and Divoky, D. *The Myth of the Hyperactive Child*, N.Y. Pantheon, 1975

Stearns, M.S., Robinson, M.L. and Thomas, T.C. "Parental Involvement in Compensatory Education Programs," in *Stanford Research Institute Report* available as ERIC No. 088588, August, 1973

Stewart, K. *Dream Theory in Malaya*, N.Y. Complex, 1951 (especially VI, 21-34)

Tway, E., ed. *Reading Ladders for Human Relations*, American Council on Education, One Dupont Circle, Washington D.C. 20036

Wald, K. *The Children of Che*, Palo Alto CA, Ramparts Press, 1968

Waxman, S. *What is a Girl? What is a Boy?* Peace Press, 3828 Willat Ave., Culver City CA 90230, 1976

Bibliography II
Some good books for young children

Adoff, A. *Black is Brown is Tan*, N.Y. Harper & Row, 1973

Andry, A.C. and Schepp, S. *How Babies are Made*, N.Y. Time-Life, 1968

Brenner, B. *Bodies*, N.Y. Dutton, 1973

Brown, M. *Goodnight Moon*, N.Y. Harper & Row, 1947

Brown, M. *Wait Till the Moon is Full*, N.Y. Harper & Row, 1948

Caines, J. *Abby*, N.Y. Harper & Row, 1973

Chess, V. and Gorey, E. *Fletcher and Zenobia*, N.Y. Meredith, 1967

Clarke, M. *Congo Boy*, Englewood Cliffs NJ, Scholastic, 1965

Freeman, D. *Corduroy*, Englewood Cliffs NJ, Scholastic, 1973

Freeman, D. *Corduroy's Pocket*, Englewood Cliffs NJ, Scholastic, 1975

Gordon, S. and J. *Did the Sun Shine Before You Were Born?* Fayetteville, NY, Ed-U Press, 1974

Haas, I. *The Maggie B*, Englewood Cliffs NJ, Scholastic, 1975

Keats, E.J. All titles, Englewood Cliffs NJ, Scholastic, c.1965

Kindred, W. *Negatu in the Garden*, N.Y. McGraw Hill, 1971

Lionni, L. All titles, N.Y. Pantheon, Scholastic, and Obolensky, c.1963

Llerena, C. *The Fair at Kanta*, N.Y. Holt, Rinehart & Winston, 1975

Mayer, M. *There's a Nightmare in My Closet*, N.Y. Dial, 1968

Merrill, J. and Scott, F.G. *How Many Kids are Hiding on My Block?* Chicago, A. Whitman, 1970

Mosel, A. *Tikki Tikki Tembo*, Englewood Cliffs NJ, Scholastic, 1968

Nilsson, L. *How Was I Born?* N.Y. Delacorte, 1975

Polland, B.K. *The Sensible Book*, Millbrae CA, Celestial Arts, 1974

Potter, B. *The Tale of Peter Rabbit*, N.Y. Warne, 1902 and Englewood Cliffs NJ, Scholastic, 1972

de Regniers, B. *Giant Story*, N.Y. Harper & Row, 1953

de Regniers, B. *May I Bring a Friend?* N.Y. Atheneum, 1974

Rey, H.A. *Curious George Rides a Bike*, Englewood Cliffs NJ, Scholastic, 1973

Scheer, J. *Rain Makes Applesauce*, N.Y. Holiday House, 1975

Scott, A.H. *On Mother's Lap*, N.Y. McGraw Hill, 1972

Scott, A.H. *Sam*, N.Y. McGraw Hill, 1967

Selsam, M. *How Kittens Grow*, Englewood Cliffs NJ, Scholastic, 1977

Sendak, M. All titles, N.Y. Harper & Row, and Scholastic, c.1970

Sheffield, M. *Where do Babies Come From?* N.Y. Knopf, 1972

Sheppard, G. *The Man Who Gave Himself Away*, N.Y. Harlin Quist, 1971

Slobodkina, E. *Caps for Sale*, Englewood Cliffs NJ, Scholastic, 1967

Stein, S. *Making Babies*, N.Y. Walker, 1974

Stevens, C. *The Birth of Sunset's Kittens*, N.Y. Young Scott, 1969

Tworkov, J. *The Camel Who Took a Walk*, N.Y. Dutton, 1951

Webber, I. *It Looks Like This*, N.Y. Young Scott, 1960. Spanish bilingual edition published by International Society for General Semantics, San Francisco, 1976

Yashima, T. *Umbrella*, N.Y. Viking Seafarer, 1970

Zolotow, C. *Mr. Rabbit and the Lovely Present*, Englewood Cliffs NJ, Scholastic, 1962

Zolotow, C. *William's Doll*, N.Y. Harper & Row, 1972

Epilog

How this book came to be written

I had known for a while that there were some stories in my head which people might find useful. But getting them down on paper seemed to be full of terrors and shadows, so I avoided writing a book until my friend, the poet Ben Moore, agreed to interview me on tape. If he hadn't encouraged me, this book wouldn't have been written.

My mother, Helen Levitov Sobell, who was getting her Ed.D. in computer education, advised me to edit my book on a computer. It seemed a good idea, but I had no experience editing or using computers, and no access to either hardware or software, so the transcript of the tapes ripened in a file drawer. Then people around me began offering resources. Ron Clemens lent me my first terminal. Later, Comer Marshall gave me one. My brother, Mark Sobell, let me keep his computer in my home for several months. Helen moved to the Bay Area, bought a computer, and shared it with me. I used resources and technical assistance from a bunch of good people: Kris Bolling, Carl Cheney, John Claydon, Pete Hollenbeck, Paul Jackson, Laura King, Pat McClung, and Karl Ramsay.

Then I began farming out pieces to people, hoping they'd encourage the project. They read raggedy writing and gave me good advice. Among them were Margaret Bean, Catherine Camp, Edwin Cerney, Carl Cheney, Grace Darling, Jim Edwards, Daria Flores, Bob and Carol Friedenberg, Casey Gurewitz, Susan Hockey, Audrey Jones, Lisbeth Jones, Donna Levis, Joan MacKenzie, Jeanne Adleman Mahoney, Lissa Matross, Ruth Messinger, Jean Pauline, Dan Safran, Shoshanna, Judith Tumin, and Sara Turnbull.

Each bit of organizing and rewriting was torture to me, and I'd have given up despite the encouragement of the readers, had Graham Prindle and Betty Schwimmer not offered to help me condense, organize and refine my stuff. We sat in the garden and turned a pile of ideas into a book with a shape. The first shape worked for about four months, and then got traded in on a second, more or less the one you have just read.

Finally we had something, but it trudged except where the children danced through, relieving my heavy style. Then Isobel Cerney, a woman whose whole life has been devoted to editing our society so that people can live caring, productive, peaceful lives, began to work with me, word by word, removing my arrogance from the text and highlighting the truth that children have taught me over the years.

Graham Prindle joined Isobel and me for a final editing of the manuscript. The book is done now and, in the process, they've taught me to write. It is a grand gift, and my thanks are never going to adequately appreciate Graham and Isobel. Anything clumsy remains because I didn't listen to them, anything graceful shows their touch. How nice, as a teacher, to find myself the student of such artists.

The moral is that non-writers like ourselves have things to say, and can find ways to say them, with help from our friends. Try it, and let me see what you come up with. Best of luck!

Index